DATE DUE			
Nov 29 '72			
Dec 15 78 B			

Black Fiddler

BLACK FIDDLER

By Richard Piro

New York  *1971*

William Morrow and Company, Inc.

To Julius R. Rubin

Photographs by Dan O'Neil IV

Printed in the United States of America by
The Colonial Press Inc., Clinton, Mass.

Library of Congress Catalog Card
Number 70-142407

INTRODUCTION

by Joseph Stein,
author of the book for
Fiddler on the Roof

I have seen *Fiddler on the Roof* perhaps a hundred times or more, under all sorts of circumstances and in numerous languages. I have lived through its formative period—the writing, the pre-production, the rehearsals, the out-of-town tryouts, the Broadway opening. I have seen productions in New York and London, Tokyo and Tel Aviv, Amsterdam and Paris. I felt I pretty much knew the sort of impact the show might have on all sorts of audiences.

But riding through the unfamiliar Brooklyn streets that night in May, on my way to a teen-age black presentation of *Fiddler,* I had no idea what to expect.

My colleagues and I had given special permission for this production because of the very unique circumstances: The neighborhood, we knew, was in turmoil following a disastrous teachers' strike; there was a good deal of hostility between the black community and the largely white, largely Jewish school staff; there were ugly rumblings of anti-Semitism in the area. A production of *Fiddler* might serve as a small tool to help heal the breach, to emphasize the parallels between the two groups, the similarities in their history, their traditions.

It took perhaps five minutes of conversation with Harold Prince, the producer, and Jerry Bock and Sheldon Harnick, writers of the musical score, for us all to agree that, despite the rigid rule forbidding amateur productions, this project deserved our support and approval.

But what sort of *Fiddler* could we expect? These were teen-agers, children totally unfamiliar with the customs, the language, the background of our play. It could be just a "cute" experience, children dressed and made up to act as grown-ups; even worse, if the young black cast had no feeling for the essence of the play, it could turn out to be a mockery, the characters they were playing could even be objects of ridicule. So it was with some concern that we entered the crowded auditorium.

But as soon as the curtain opened, and the young black Tevye started his monologue, I knew, we all knew, that this would be a unique theatrical experience. "A fiddler on the roof," he began. "Sounds crazy, no? But in our little village of Anatevka you might say every one of us is a fiddler on the roof. . . ." And it didn't sound crazy at all! The boy meant it, and felt it. Fake beard, black face and all, he was an old Jew in the shtetl, telling us honestly how he felt about his lot. And as the rest of the company joined him, they too had been transformed into the people of Anatevka, reflecting their sadness, their warmth, their humor.

From an objective, critical point of view, I suppose, it was not a particularly great performance. These were, after all, teen-agers and amateurs attempting very difficult roles. It was something else. These black children from the slums of Brownsville truly believed themselves to be Jews in the ghetto of old Russia. And because they believed, the audience believed and was deeply moved.

It was hard to understand how this came about—it could not simply be a matter of coaching and rehearsing, for where would that inner feeling come from?—until I read Richard Piro's account of the experience.

Black Fiddler is not really about the preparation of the production of *Fiddler*. It is that, of course, but it is a great deal more than that.

It is a very revealing personal testament. Mr. Piro tells of his problems, his travails, his anguish, his triumphs, and his joy with complete honesty, slated with gutsy humor. He does not spare himself, and we get to know a man with an overdose of courage, strength, and fierce loyalty, matched by an equally large portion of arrogance, or more accurately (since he was dealing with a Jewish theme) "chutzpah." A fascinating, irritating, thoroughly delightful fellow.

It is an excellent sociological document. I have read nothing purporting to describe life in a ghetto school to equal *Black Fiddler* in giving the reader a sense of being there. The kids, the teachers, the community are all alive. It is frightening, it is sad, it is real, and above all, it is human. There are no statistics in this book, just people, children and adults, black and white, being damaged by a mindless educational system.

It is an exciting suspense story, complete with its heroes and villains, its small and large crises, its climax and denouement. I happened to have played a part in the story (a bit part, really; a few small scenes) so I knew some of it. But the story of this production, from its uneasy start to its shaky opening night (which, by comparison, made the traditional difficulties of getting a musical to Broadway feel ridiculously easy), still had genuine drama.

And above all, it is a love story, a love story of the rarest kind. Without any self-consciousness, it tells of the love between a teacher and his pupils, a love which helped each of them to know each other and to know themselves. It is not sentimental; Mr. Piro and his kids understand each other too well for that. They get irritated, they get angry, they get frustrated, but they do know and do trust and do love each other.

And finally, as the epilogue shows, it has elements of tragedy . . . not just for Mr. Piro, or for the students of Junior High School 275, but for all of us.

But *Black Fiddler* does leave us with a residue of hope. In his final memo to his cast and crew, Mr. Piro wrote that as a result of the production, "Lots and lots of people have different ideas about blacks and Jews and human relations . . . and one of the most exciting results is the fact that our community now shares our deep belief that the boys and girls of our school are first-class citizens of the world, capable of delivering first-class contributions to society." If I may paraphrase *Fiddler,* "From your mouth, Mr. Piro, to God's ears."

INTRODUCTION

by Major Owens,
Commissioner of the New York City Community Development Agency and former Executive Director of the Brownsville Community Council

Black Fiddler should be required reading for people who want to begin to understand the problems of the schools in our poverty-oppressed Black and Puerto Rican communities. The volumes of statistics and reports already available about schools like Junior High School 275 and communities like Brownsville, Brooklyn, tell only a limited story. To understand to any significant degree one must become involved in some specific, concrete undertaking. Since most of us will never have the opportunity for this kind of direct personal involvement, I recommend reading a collection of deeply felt individual accounts, starting with *Black Fiddler*.

In the fall of 1968 insurmountable barriers were solidly constructed between the community and the schools. The UFT strike with its massive over-kill propaganda bombed out all bridges between parents and teachers. The first chapter of *Black Fiddler* relates the beginning of a new era of vicious warfare between the community and the schools. The UFT made hundreds of thousands of photo-offset copies of anti-Semitic leaflets originally handwritten by obvious cranks.

This specter of anti-Semitism, claimed by many to be a UFT invention to guarantee a victory over the Ocean Hill school complex, initiated a downward spiral which made the opposition of the Jewish teachers to the children's *Fiddler* as inevitable as the later stoning of the school by angry high school youth.

To fully understand the forces at work in *Black Fiddler* it is also important to remember the history of J.H.S. 275. This school was born amidst a stormy controversy which involved integrationists from all over the city. A long, bitter battle was waged on the picket lines and in the courts to achieve a zoning for the school which would promote maximum integration. It is ironic that the hostile Black power advocates who depress and anger Piro in the closing pages of the book happen to be the community descendants of parents who begged for total integration.

Piro is not a politician or an antipoverty social engineer. He is an artist focusing on a specific concrete, complex chunk of life. In his book we live through an important symbolic episode in the life of the New York City school system without being distracted by sociological analysis or political commentary. We are presented with an opportunity to understand a complex interplay of forces by living through it all in sympathy and empathy with an exciting gathering of heroes and heroines. Among them are Frances Brown, the community representative who delivers an address on art as a tool for achieving understanding between groups to superficial and insensitive teachers. And there's Teddy Smith who leads this *Fiddler* out of the category of student production into a realm of its own and emerges as a symbol of the ghetto student burdened with personal problems but nevertheless a gold mine of talent and ability. And the principal, Allen Robbins, who is a rare administrator with a soul who uses his bureaucratic cleverness not to hinder but to facilitate creativity.

As the leading man, Piro is fortunate to have a good supporting cast, but there should be no doubt that he is the star. His stubborn perseverance and his capacity to take persecution make this an inspiring story. Piro's self-portrait is generally a critical one. In several situations he pointedly illustrates why he should not be the guy who leads the human relations seminar or who represents his country at the UN. Diplomacy is not one of Piro's strengths, and for this weakness he is made to suffer in addition to the usual suffering forced upon those who are sensitive and creative. Piro's unique genius lies in his ability to develop individuals and groups and to keep them focused on a meaningful task.

The failure of individual courage and a sense of responsibility is a recurring concern of *Black Fiddler*. Apathy and acquiescence emerge as the evil and the sickness plaguing both the primitive and the very decadent. The teachers who sit silently by in the lunchroom while Piro is almost attacked by an angry racist colleague are as despicable as the local residents who ignore Piro's desperate struggle with a subway mugger. After a long vacation, Piro, forgetting that artists can't go home again, returned to a J.H.S. 275 from which all courage seems to have fled. In all of the schools and outside in the larger community of Brownsville where the problems are of staggering immensity, the courage to resist the easy dramatic answers and stay with the hard detailed work of unraveling the knots which bind a neighborhood is still a prime need.

On the surface Brownsville appears to be a place where the forces of construction are still losing to the forces of demolition. My last visit to Brownsville—I often go home again—was to attend a ground-breaking ceremony for a new community-sponsored housing complex a few blocks from J.H.S. 275. Discussions with old friends confirmed my belief that this physical rebuilding was symbolic of something deeper happening within the community. I am convinced that here is a special Anatevka that can never be uprooted and swept away.

Piro and the performance of *Fiddler* are now a part of an evolving community culture; the battle to produce a show takes its place alongside numerous other battles against the system. For the school, the community, and for New York City, Piro produced a moment of excellence and magic. As an artist he rose to the challenge of the medium before him. Producing a play in Scarsdale or Darien will never place similar tests on his genius as artist and teacher. With mixed emotions we accept Piro's resignation and forego the production of *Man of La Mancha.* We will have to wait for one of his inspired students who will have many advantages, including the opportunity to read *Black Fiddler.* The student will also be Black and probably filled with the sense of mission of his generation. Unlike his teacher, he will probably enjoy more group support. But should this optimistic prediction fail, the example of *Black Fiddler* will still inspire: Regardless of the size of the problem, each individual can seize the challenge of that which is immediately before him, fight the little unbeatable foes as they arise, and persevere to get as close as possible to the realization of some small but impossible dream.

1

"It took me six weeks to learn these words," declared Duane McCullars, the thirteen-year-old Dromio, "and this audience is goin' to understand every damn one of 'em."

He raced to his first-scene position. The curtain parted. The play began. Shortly afterwards Duane shot me a despairing glance from the stage. Noise being produced by young toilet-seekers in combination with parental threats of "C'mon right back now, y'heah?" all but obliterated what we had hoped would be a hilarious script. It *was* Shakespeare—visually impressive—but incredibly dull without the lines being heard. When they were taking their final bows, the two teenage Dromios decided that "Naught but tragedie enlargeth the bladder," and suggested our play be renamed *The Errors of Comedy*. Summer school '68 was over.

Half an hour after the curtain came down, I was on my way to Puerto Rico for a rest. On September third, a week later, I returned to New York City ready to face my first day of school for the tenth consecutive year.

Teacher-orientation day at Harry A. Eiseman Junior High School 275 in Brownsville, Brooklyn, began as it did in all other New York City schools, with a renewal of teacher friendships. The morning continued with department chairmen frantically looking for their lost new teachers, mock department meetings which discussed everything but curriculum, card playing in the faculty room, basketball games in the gym, and later, of course, a grand faculty conference. The highlight—it kept seasoned teachers from taking an extra day's vacation—was collecting the August salary checks after an hour-long wait in line. The least pleasant task involved rescuing classrooms from the ravages of summer cleaning, which meant replacement of desks, chairs, bulletin boards, pianos, music stands, flags, and wall decorations to their proper locations. A treat was uncrating new teaching materials delivered during the summer recess. No children were allowed into the building, although many gathered outside to gape at the new beards, moustaches, Afro hairstyles, miniskirts and occasionally to hail an old teacher-friend from last June.

We were all relieved when the staff was finally brought to order by the principal. Instead of delivering the annual "I-hope-you-all-had-a-restful-summer-and-are-ready-for-work" speech, Dr. Allen Robbins surprised us with an emotionally charged indictment of the New York City school system and its consistent failure to serve all the needs of all the children. "As principal of a black and Puerto Rican ghetto junior high school, I pledge to you a year of severe accountability during which no teacher is to expect administrative support of unprofessional conduct. This community is on the march to have a greater voice in the internal operations of its schools," Dr. Robbins said, "and I, for one, most heartily welcome this long overdue innovation."

His address was refreshingly spontaneous, a quality that was rare with inner-city school administrators. As a music and drama teacher with productions of *The Crucible, Fiddler on the Roof, Ceremony of Carols,* and *Testament of*

Freedom ready for immediate rehearsal, I was not threatened by this community's determination to upgrade education for its children.

When I could no longer tolerate the vacuum of a school without children, I punched out at 2:30 P.M., half an hour earlier than duty required. A light rain fell as I boarded the bus to ride the five blocks to the subway where I could catch a train bound to Manhattan and home. While paying the bus fare I realized I had only two dollars in cash. I removed one dollar in preparation for buying subway tokens and, not wishing to struggle with damp clothes and tight trousers, put the wallet into my briefcase. I ran a quick calculation on how to make the bank in time to deposit the twelve hundred dollars in checks I had received that afternoon, for normal August teacher salary as well as the summer-school extra pay. My destination also included a midtown jeweler to look at wristwatches, since mine had just stopped running for the fourth time. Then, with no more to think about, I opened a novel, the last of the *Mandingo* series, and tuned out everything around me.

The bus reached the elevated station. I picked up the briefcase and readied the dollar for tokens. At the corner I nodded, as I had many times before, to several people who hung around the doughnut shop. Then I started up the stairs, something I had been doing for three years in the afternoon and late at night after concerts, performances, and PTA affairs.

At the top of the stairs I turned left and started walking down a short passageway, about ten yards long, which ended with a right turn, just a few feet from the token booth. On one side were broken windows that looked out on the street; on the other side were iron grillwork and, beyond, the set of stairs which led up to the train platform.

I was almost within sight of the token booth when someone behind me gripped my wrist. Still holding onto the briefcase, I involuntarily turned around. Facing me was a black man in his middle or late twenties, very dark, with tiny bloodshot eyes peering from beneath a large forehead. He growled, "Give me your money. All of it!" My first reaction was to ignore the threat and concentrate on the fact that the smell of alcohol on his breath indicated he wasn't a drug addict desperate for a "fix." Since this was one of only two possible entrances to the subway, I felt somewhat secure that somebody would soon pass by. As calmly as possible I said, "Excuse me, what did you say?"

As my assailant released my wrist his other hand swung forward holding a long knife, more ugly than sinister. He pushed me into the grillwork and pressed the blade against my throat, breaking the skin. He repeated his demand and increased the pressure of the knife. At that moment several black men and a black woman walked up the stairs and passed us. Over my assailant's shoulder I watched their nervous glances followed by a too-casual air of unconcern. I waited, listening to them purchase their tokens, pass through the turnstiles, and walk upstairs to the train platform. Several blacks passed us coming down on the other side of the grille. No alarm was given.

Real physical danger heightens perception, and several thought fragments rushed through my mind: I was absolutely certain I was about to be murdered. I was not afraid. I wondered why I was not afraid.

I held out the dollar bill. Ignoring the money, the mugger further increased the pressure of the knife against my throat. I thought, "Goddammit, I'm not going to die without a struggle for two lousy dollars!" I grabbed his knife arm while shouting for help. He wrenched his arm free and drove the knife into the small of my back, just over a kidney, with enough force to throw me to the side.

"I don't have any more money!" I screamed. New thought

fragments: It doesn't hurt. Why am I still conscious? Still no real terror but a kind of fear-embarrassment.

He continued stabbing. By this time my shirt was ripped off, my pockets torn out, and we were wrestling on the greasy, rain-slick concrete floor. After what seemed a long time (it was probably less than three minutes), he spotted the briefcase and moved to get it. I was not concerned with the summer-work checks because I knew I could stop payment on them immediately. It was having to face the red tape of the Board of Education Payroll Division and—more important—the loss of a ten-year-old address book plus a production portfolio for *Fiddler on the Roof*. I jumped up and ran after him.

We grappled at the top of the stairs. I was now in a state of hysteria; my intent was to throw both of us down the stairs headfirst. I was conscious of blood but felt no physical pain in spite of the stabs and blows.

I was angry, too, with the people hanging about the coffee shop below the stairs. For the past three years I had been taking students into that shop almost every day for general bull sessions. The hang-abouts knew well who and what I was. Frequently our discussions were interrupted with, "You listen to that man, y'hear? He help you get out of here." From the top of the stairs I caught a glimpse of these same people standing in silence, watching the struggle with mild interest.

Finally, without the briefcase or the initial dollar bill, the mugger fled down the stairs and into the crowd, which parted politely for him. I watched as he held up his arm to examine the blood streaming from his hand. Then I realized why I was still conscious. Every time he had stabbed directly, the blade had jackknifed, badly cutting his own hand. I was covered with cuts and scratches but no punctures, except the small one on my throat. He melted into the crowd.

With full realization of the ridiculousness of the pose I was assuming, shirt torn off and covered with blood, I leaned over the railing and, looking down at the unconcerned black faces of my "friends," shouted, "Thanks! Thanks a fucking lot." No reaction. Silence.

I picked up my nylon jacket, put it on, and walked to the token booth with no specific aim in mind except to get out of there as quickly as possible. Reflexively I asked, "Is there a policeman around?" but I had no plans to remain until one could be summoned. Almost immediately a black Transit Authority officer appeared behind me, stating he had just come off duty. He asked for a description of the mugger.

"I know he was colored," he said. "But what did he have on?"

I concentrated on the dark complexion, electric-lime-colored trousers, and new gray snakeskin shoes. The policeman dashed down the stairs.

I looked up to see Sam Wells, one of the students who was closest to me, observing the scene from the other side of the turnstiles. I prepared an oh-it's-nothing smile. He pushed through the turnstile and, obviously embarrassed, said, "Hello, Mr. Piro." With a sly grin he started down the steps on his way home. The policeman returned with two drunk and confused black men, neither wearing green pants. I apologized and they were dismissed.

After completing an interminably long report (I had to spell each word) the officer insisted I wait for an ambulance from the local hospital. I thought to myself, "Fuck you, baby, and have to make this same trip in the dark?"

His final question was, "Are you sure you don't want to press charges?"

"Against what," I shouted to myself, "the conditions that reduced this creature to such an act?"

My right earlobe was cut and bleeding. I had deep knife scratches all over my back and shoulders. My throat was bleeding and pain stabbed at my ribs when I took a breath.

The forty-five-minute train ride was made with my mind numb. I couldn't afford to think, but kept repeating to myself, "It doesn't matter. It doesn't matter."

It was difficult to acknowledge having been stupid. Stupid because, being a few feet away from the token attendant's view when my wrist was grabbed, I could easily have moved forward. Stupid because I thought people would help me. Stupid because I was so totally blanked out by reading the novel that had I so much as glanced around I would have seen the intent of the mugger and quickened my pace. Stupid because I didn't try to hurt him. Stupid because I felt I had earned the right to safe passage in that neighborhood.

At Fourteenth Street on Manhattan's West Side, I got off the train and started walking up Seventh Avenue. Turning west on Sixteenth Street, I passed my own building and continued down the block to the house of my friend Joe Sicari.

Joe and I had met as eighth-graders in a Catholic high school in Cambridge, Massachusetts, and our friendship continued growing for the next twenty years. A professional actor, he had served as a theater conscience during my eight years of teaching in and around New York City. If he were home, fine; if not, I would wait.

I opened his door with my key; as usual, he was talking on the telephone. I stepped in quietly and stood behind him at the sofa, expressionless but fully aware of how this scene would take on camera. I waited. He sensed a break from routine visiting and looked up.

"My God," he shouted into the phone. "My best friend just came in and he's covered with blood!" Rapidly he described my condition in detail. Finally he asked me what happened, and as I described the events, he repeated each fact into the phone, with embellishments. In the same instant we both realized the ridiculous theatricality of the situation and burst into laughter. He hung up and started to make coffee, all the while shifting from concern for my well-being to fury at "those fucking bastards out there who have to live in such fear."

I sat down and tried listening to what he thought I was feeling. It wasn't working. He stopped. Assuming a different role, he sat opposite me on the piano bench and said, "You know, Dick, it's about time you faced up to what's really going on out there."

"Like what?" (I knew what he meant.)

"I mean like your whole involvement with that school, that ghetto, and blacks in general. It's sick."

"Joe, this is hardly the time to . . ."

"No. We are going to talk about it right now. For the past four years I've seen you totally reverse roles, so that it's you needing them rather than them needing you. When people rave on about how dedicated you are to teaching, what do you feel?"

"OK. I feel embarrassed because I know that I'm taking more from the kids than I'm giving. No. Not exactly that but what I give to the kids is matched trade for trade with what I take."

"What exactly does 'dedication' mean to you?"

"Well . . ."

"Never mind 'well,' I want a fast answer."

"It means being concerned only with giving, without any anticipated rewards. That's not where it's at for me."

"Dick, what are you feeling right now—I don't mean the physical pain—in your head?"

"Guilt."

"How?"

"I know that you're going to scream that I'm sick again, but I feel so guilty for that poor miserable son of a bitch out there on the subway. What a terrible mistake he made. We really failed that one in his seventh grade."

"What's the worst thing that can happen now?"

"That I won't go back to Brooklyn."

"And they need you, right?"

"I need them, too, remember?"

"If they need you so very much, why didn't any of those people help you or, at least, give an alarm?"

"They were afraid to."

"Bullshit! All they saw was whitey getting messed on by one of the brothers."

"That too; but I think that idea simply gives them an excuse not to face up to their own fear."

"Something else is going on in your head. What is it?"

"You know . . . I'm kind of proud—which reminds me that I'm going to call up Dr. Robbins."

"Only you could manage to muster up pride out of—"

"Hey, Joe, wait a minute! For years the teachers have been begging me not to go home that way and I wouldn't listen. But the worst happened and I survived. Now I can sport full credentials of working in a black ghetto."

Joe threw up his hands in despair as I dialed Dr. Robbins and informed him of the mugging. "If it can happen to *you,*" he said, shocked and disgusted, "then there isn't the ghost of a chance for any of us working in this building."

It was Thursday. That evening the United Federation of Teachers called a general strike in support of the nineteen teachers refused admittance to their classes in a nearby school by a black demonstration-school project administrator. The face of that administrator—Rhody McCoy—became the face of my mugger and I struck gladly. The weekend and subsequent two-day strike gave me five days to build up a terror of that staircase and that subway entrance.

The two-day mini-strike ended and we returned to work on Wednesday with enough *if*s hanging over the City to insure another, much longer, work stoppage. On the first morning of school I took a loaded starter pistol from my collection of theatrical props and put it in my jacket pocket, never taking my hand off it until I punched in.

I arranged to have the drama class come to my Manhattan apartment for daily rehearsals during the expected strike.

Excitement permeated the air. For many teachers it was an opportunity to strike back at what they felt was the encroaching and unfair power given to black leaders by the Board of Education. For the children it meant an extended summer recess. For me it was the delicious anticipation of working with children on a professional-theater time schedule.

For three years our pattern had been to produce a midwinter one-act play followed by a major musical in the spring, using the eighth-grade drama majors—thirty or so fourteen-to-sixteen-year-olds. During the musical's preparation period, the finished one-act production toured the schools in the neighborhood, thus keeping the cast at a performing level. However, this year we intended a change. It was high time the drama department grew to its full potential. To do this, I selected a major four-act play—Arthur Miller's *The Crucible*—for the midwinter opener. The magnitude of the project was frightening but not impossible. Most of the cast had received individual training in improvisation through a specially funded evening center the previous year. Many had followed up this experience by appearing in the summer production of *The Comedy of Errors.* After Shakespeare and Miller, I expected to breeze through *Fiddler on the Roof,* which was not scheduled for rehearsals until after Christmas vacation. If the impending strike provided us with five daily hours of solid rehearsing outside of the normal academic environment, then I looked forward to it as a gift from the Muses. It was a once-in-a-career opportunity.

A battle plan was immediately submitted to the children. It met with hearty approval from the parents and condemnation from the militant strike-supporters, who considered it a scab activity.

That Thursday and Friday between strikes was spent both in frantic drama activity and terrible dread of the trip home after school.

I already had planned to take a leave of absence at the end of the year. Giving in to fear, I moved up the date and set about making arrangements to find a Greek island, ignoring the plans I had made with the students. I bought the plane tickets and telephoned Dr. Robbins to say good-bye, expecting his approval but hoping he wouldn't give it. He spoke fast. Logic began to quiet the growing terror. "You've been walking home that way for four years," he said, "and have never been attacked, nor have you seen such an incident. It was an accident that you were mugged."

His assistant, Mrs. Amelia Brown, took another approach: "Dick, we're going to need you when this strike is all over."

"That rope you're throwing out to save me, Amelia, is going to turn into a noose. You know that, don't you?"

"What do you mean?"

"I'm just another human being out there."

"Well. . . ?"

"I mean I'm just another *white man!*"

"I'm white, too," Amelia said.

"But, dammit, I thought I could get away with it. I've never let color have anything to do with my work. But suddenly it's become everything. I've been preaching black militancy for years. I felt totally immune to any kind of anti-white violence."

The following day I related the mugging incident to the drama class, including Sam Wells's refusal to offer aid. I did not use his name, but the children all knew who I was talking about since he had immediately broadcast an exaggerated story of what he had seen. At the end of my deliberately theatrical presentation, I glanced in Sam's direction. There were tears rolling down his face. It was enough.

What a relief it was to go on strike the next day! And a relief to remain out on strike for close to three months. During daily rehearsals with the children, I saw only a group of children that, simply, it was fun to be with. The youngsters were on fire with their roles. I postponed trying to reconcile my love-hate conflicts and concentrated on the work I do best—children and theater. We gorged on sour deli-pickles, worked furiously on characterizations, prepared group lunches in my tiny kitchen, sang, laughed, danced, and roamed through Greenwich Village; and shortly our love affair was again going full steam ahead.

2

Four months before I was mugged and prior to the teacher strikes, student, staff, and community feelings concerning Junior High School 275 were those of joyful shock and disbelief. It was the beginning of May and we had just closed the run of our first Broadway major musical—*Oliver!*—with cheers and tears.

This project was launched with Dr. Robbins' warning, "I don't think this community is going to appreciate or accept a play wherein its black children are taught to be thieves under the expert instruction of a Jew." The show nearly crashed a week before opening when a group of militant Jewish teachers unsuccessfully attempted a boycott on the grounds of its having an anti-Semitic character, Fagin. The stage was well set for another black-Jewish confrontation.

Oliver! went on as scheduled to packed houses, because of rather than in spite of the controversy. The apathetic eighty percent of the community took note of the fact that something had happened that upset a number of teachers. What was to have been just another junior-high spring show turned into a major event.

After the performance I walked out of the building overwhelmed with feelings which I could not comfortably define. As was my custom following each public performance, I wrote an open letter to the cast.

May 5, 1968 (7 P.M. Sunday Night)
TO: Cast & Crew of Oliver!
FROM: R. J. Piro
SUBJECT: Love Power

I have just seen my mother off on her broom to Boston. All weekend I have looked forward to writing this letter to you and objected to every minute I had to entertain la mama. Now that I'm free to think on it, I don't know what to say. I am terribly tired and terribly depressed. Last Friday was—well—last Friday was everything; everything I have ever read, thought, studied, taught, and hoped. I was a little boy again, dreaming of being a teacher; and, as in Twilight Zone, that dream was taking place right before my eyes. May I cite one example? When the wires snapped and I saw that 300-pound piece of scenery fall I almost didn't care (as soon as I saw that nobody was hurt). I had no doubt whatsoever that the show would go on without missing more than 2 beats. In other words, you all had so gained my respect for your abilities (cast AND crew) that I trusted you to recover instantly. As I reread this, it sounds too simple. A voice says, "So you trusted them—big deal!" It is a big deal! To gain trust and respect from anyone is about the biggest deal any one of us can hope for—and you have this from me. Add a little love and you have about all you can get. You can respect without love, love without respect and trust with or without either. I offer you all three.

A teacher is a leader and sometimes a pusher. Our job is to bring you to the brink of experience. Beyond this point we must leave you and hope we have prepared you to take your own strong steps. In no area of teaching is this idea more pronounced than in music-theater. Friday night I lost all personal identification with Oliver! and simply became the poor piano player and a member of the audience. Only you and I will ever know how many, many things that happened on that stage were the result of your OWN invention and talent. I gave you "A" and "B" but YOU put them together and formed a triumphant "C." I bowed out at the last rehearsal on Wednesday and you bowed in on Thursday. How I wish the world could see your show and then share with me the idea that you are real people!

So closed the 1967–1968 season. We were on top of the world with unlimited horizons. The kids had proven beyond all doubt (even mine) that they were capable of professional quality. Bruce Birnel, the technical director, proved there was no theatrical problem beyond our equipment and imagination. The Ocean Hill–Brownsville community had seen its children functioning at maximum capacity. We—the children and I—stood in awe of each other. We had *done* it!

Before the final curtain had dropped, the dread question was asked: "Mr. Piro, what are we going to do next year?"

Sets were struck, lights taken down, props returned to their sources and costumes neatly folded and mothballed for storage. Once again the auditorium became a vacuum.

Contrary to what I had been taught, closing a successful show had never before been depressing. It was now. After eight years during which I had meticulously preplanned each project, I was stuck for the next season's musical. The agony of indecision took its toll from the excitement and joy I should have been experiencing after the successful *Oliver!* run.

The end-of-the-period buzzer announced lunch. I wasn't hungry but I felt an urgent need to be with Dr. Robbins. Using the briefcase as a spear, I forced myself through the flood of yelling children. An impasse formed as one grade attempted an exit through another grade's entrance to the student cafeteria. Several students fell into step with me, hoping to escape the lunchroom supervision. Their intent was to remain in the stairwells, cutting class for the afternoon. I shook them off and entered the faculty room.

As usual, the din was one to match the students'. Dr. Robbins was sitting alone at a corner table.

One of the advantages of sitting with the boss was that I could bring the conversation around to theater, a subject he enjoyed. Here was a man whom I admired almost to the point of embarrassment. Yet, after four years together, our strict principal-teacher relationship was still that and no more. The mutual respect was so great that we feared risking a quasi-social involvement.

He looked distracted, which is to say he was trying to look interested in his surroundings; but it was obvious he was seeing nothing but his own thoughts. As usual he was dressed in a suit and tie so outstandingly conservative that they appeared close to flamboyant. Because of his sensitivity about his short stature—he was around five feet, six inches tall—he always sat erect. It was this carriage which might have made his clothes seem more like those of a model than those of a junior-high principal. It was something other than the graying temples and the ghost of a smile he wore when distracted that made me see him as a photograph from a 1930s yearbook over the caption "Our beloved Principal" written in flowing, elegant script. He was a professional cynic and the best devil's advocate in the business, possibly because he was ashamed of his high ideals and their failure to materialize in his more than twenty years of ghetto education. When making a proposal, it was impossible to overwhelm him with excitement and enthusiasm. He had the kind of mind which absorbed details and separated them from projections. His special talent was to seize on that one overlooked triviality which in the end might upset the most carefully laid plan. It was also impossible ever to be sure, initially, where he stood on a proposed idea. He would fight your request sentence by sentence and, armed with your defense, go on to sell it to his own superiors. I loved this man.

I pulled out a chair and took off my jacket. He smiled a hello and said, "You know, Dick, I hold a doctorate from New York University and I'm mother and father to eighteen hundred kids and one hundred and five teachers. So I start to feel like I'm really somebody, and then I find *this* in my coat pocket." He unrolled a slip of paper and read in a monotone, "One quart of milk, one dozen eggs, some oranges, and don't forget to mail the letters." Dutifully I presented my stage laugh, but another clue to the man fell into place and I was embarrassed lest he see my thoughts of Claire, his wife. He saw it anyway and beamed one of his evil smiles. Then he asked, "Well, young fella, what's the spring musical proposal for next year?" Now it was my turn to squirm.

"I don't know," I said. "Goddammit, I'm stuck. With every light Bruce Birnel takes down he asks the same questions. The kids keep asking. Their parents keep calling. The teachers want to know."

"Doesn't that make you feel good?"

"Feel good? You have to be joking, and I'm in no mood . . ."

"Did it ever dawn on you that before *Oliver!* none of these people could have cared less about your plans?"

"Yes it did, and it makes the situation that much harder to take."

"How?"

"Well, what do you think it must feel like to get to this point and then just dry up?"

"I don't think it's a case of drying up as much as of having too stringent a set of requirements."

"I know it's stupid to ask, but have you any suggestions?"

His eyes twinkled with the deliciousness of the problem, and he meekly suggested, "I wish you'd give some more thought to *The Music Man*. I really like that show."

We'd been through this discussion before.

"Dr. Robbins," I said, "*The Music Man* is about a lisping little boy who is cured through playing a cornet under a fake music teacher in Iowa at the turn of the century. I'm sure our black and Puerto Rican kids will have deep identification with the script."

"Well, how about *The King and I*? My wife's fifth grade did it last year and everybody loved it."

"I hope you're playing."

"No, I'm serious."

"Look, Bruce and I don't do assembly-type shows with crepe-paper costumes and butcher-paper scenery. I refuse to get involved with any theater piece that I couldn't guarantee won't be better than anyone else has done it before in any medium."

"What do you mean?" he asked.

"I mean that I'm in competition not only with every other junior high school in the city but with any professional or amateur group that thinks it's doing real theater."

"But *The King and I* is—"

"Can you get me three thousand dollars to dress it up? If

you can I'll consider it. If not, even you must know that in spite of the opulent setting it's still on the wrong edge of boredom."

He shook his head. I was his private white elephant. There are enough problems with a special-service ghetto junior high school without the added difficulties of a theater department out of all proportion to the rest of the curriculum. For years the school had functioned well; then in blew "Hurricane Piro." After some excursions into classical theater (Shakespeare and Molière) the community decided that our school was the showcase of Brownsville ("They do *Shakespeare!*"). Some of the teaching staff were sullen and angry. Too much budget and scheduling emphasis went into the music and drama program and a certain amount of antagonism lay just beneath the surface of professional courtesy. There were many who, although they appreciated our successes, would have felt more secure if we had failed once in a while. Several times a day they asked Dr. Robbins, "How come the music guys always get what they want? What is this, a damn conservatory?"

Against great odds, including lack of support from the Board of Education, we had initiated an annual project wherein up to two hundred music and drama students took a four-day trip to live with and perform for the all-white community of Somerset, Massachusetts. The parents were proud of this event and indicated their trust in the department by placing the physical welfare of their children in our hands.

Teachers in the other departments felt left out. Yet, as a public-relations arm, the annual concerts and shows attracted hundreds of people who thus evaluated the school in music-drama terms only. There were community rumblings about the contradiction between kids who were supposedly unable to read doing serious justice to three Shakespearean productions. In the middle of these conflicts sat one Dr. Allen Robbins who, while appreciating what he had, must have occasionally wished he didn't have the source of aggravation that the constant demand for excellence brought.

Just then Bruce Birnel placed his tray on our table. Bruce was a mixed grille and enjoyed a unique place on the staff. His license was in music and his training was at Juilliard School of Music in New York. His major source of income was playing in and booking dance bands for Jewish affairs. His chief value to the school was in the area of audio-visual arts, which meant maintenance of cameras, tape recorders, overhead projectors, and countless other machines including the school's public address system. He was twenty-eight years old and looked thirty-five. He attacked his interests with a vengeance, and his work on our shows constituted sixty percent of their professionalism. His lighting work was brilliant.

Bruce took off his deep-aqua-colored watered-silk sport coat and gave full display to his raspberry-colored shirt and huge onyx cufflinks. Dr. Robbins looked up and said,

"So how's our genius-with-the-lights today?"

"I could be a lot better if Piro would come down from his *Oliver!* high and give me a script for next spring."

"You son of a bitch," I said.

Bruce broke the tension with, "Hey gang, I've got a fantastic idea! Listen. David Merrick's making a fortune with his black company of *Hello, Dolly!* Why don't we do a black *Fiddler on the Roof?*"

We laughed, Robbins the hardest.

"First, Bruce," I said, "you should know by now that I won't cast on color, so a black *Fiddler* doesn't turn me on. And neither does a white one. I've seen that show four times and still feel cheated."

Dr. Robbins sat up.

"After a fantastic opening," I continued, "the show sinks into Broadway floss with fancy-schmancy Jerome Robbins dancing and pseudo-ethnic crap. Sorry. *Fiddler* is out of the running."

A sly smile from Robbins. "OK, just what are you looking for in a script?"

"Yeah," Bruce mimicked, "whaddya want from us?"

"OK, I'm ready for this gang-up. I'm about to preach and demand complete attention."

"Oh, God," Bruce moaned. "We got ourselves into a sermon."

I ignored Bruce's facetiousness and was encouraged by Robbins' curious scrutiny.

"We cannot ever lose sight of the fact that in drama we have more and better tools for getting to kids *and* their parents. What should we be doing in school? I'll tell you, since you asked. Our job is human relations; not music, or drama, or math, or reading. I must feel—no, have a certainty—that the kids in the cast, the kids in the audiences, *and* mommy and daddy will walk away from performances closer to the strangers they sat with. I know what you're going to say, Bruce, but you don't have to."

Bruce said it anyway, because he thought it was clever. "If you want to run a damn clinic, go to work in a hospital. We're in show business."

Dr. Robbins moved in. "All right, Dick, what were the 'clinical' aspects of your *Oliver!*?"

"Touché, boss. You did it again! I don't really know. Since it was our first major Broadway musical I wanted something immediately appealing in order to prove the entertainability of our kids on a professional level. It had to grab fast."

At that moment, Irene Seitzer, guidance counselor and an articulate conscience of the school, made her steamroller entrance. She had been listening to our conversation and, characteristic of her drive to clarify and simplify, albeit in psychological jargon, she joined us.

"Come on, Richard, don't be so humble! You know what *Oliver!* was about and why it had such tremendous impact on the audiences."

I stifled a smile, because she was about to do one of her "bits" and I loved seeing this close friend in action. Dr. Robbins lifted his chin, obviously aware of Irene's six-foot height.

"No, Irene, I don't know," I teased. "You always come up with great motivations for my shows after they close. What's this one?"

"OK," she said. "Who's the most sympathetic character in the play?"

Bruce immediately answered, "Oliver?"

"Nonsense! It was Fagin and you all know it. With absolutely no contact with the establishment—in fact he's anti-establishment—he is the only character who exhibits any sympathy or real feeling for the orphans on the streets. Do any of you have any idea what social conditions for the London poor were at that time? What did the establishment do for the kids? They starved them, worked them like slaves. In other words, those who were getting paid to perform social action were involved only in exploitation. Fagin exploited the kids, granted, but he also gave a great deal of love and—yes—respect to them. It may not have presented your 'message,' Richard, but as a microcosm of what goes on in our kids' lives in Brownsville, *Oliver!* was very much where it is at right now, at least to the kids."

Bruce grinned. "Hey, Richard, did you know all that before? How come you never told me?"

"Because Irene says it so much better than I do. She's my voice of reason."

"Richard," Irene shot in, "what character did you identify with in *Oliver!*? No thinking. I want a fast answer."

"Why, Fagin, of course. Who am I to blow your argument?"

Robbins was enjoying the banter and asked, "OK, Mrs. Smarts, what was the human-relations theme of Piro's *Taming of the Shrew*?"

Irene took a fast swallow of her cottage cheese and, before she got the teacup to her mouth, shot back, "The classic male-female roles as defined by the traditional Judeo-Christian ethic."

She was performing on cue, comfortably and sincerely. It was familiar territory. I loved her, especially when she was like this. For the first time during the period I began to relax.

"Remember," she went on, "our kids come from a matriarchal society where the woman has castrated the male to the point where no intelligent girl would think of marrying this creature she has created—the nonfunctioning male. She's not to blame, though, because basic survival dictated that someone had to procure food and shelter. White America made opportunities possible only for the black woman. Didn't you watch the audiences during *Taming of the Shrew*? They were spellbound watching that guy bully the girl. It was every black male child's dream of being a man. Richard's a showman first, but he also has an uncanny sense of what works for this community."

"Hey, Irene, you're making me into—"

She wasn't about to be interrupted. "*Romeo and Juliet* had an obvious human-relations theme, but the Molière was tricky. At the third performance I caught on. *That Scoundrel Scapin* was all involved with the little guy who, in spite of being of the servant class, managed to overcome the establishment. This meant that those who inherited leadership didn't deserve it or, at least, didn't have the brains for it. Our kids had instant identity with Scapin's outsmarting all those stuffy old nobles. I'm somewhat familiar with Richard's Italian background in Boston, and I suspect there was a lot of him in Scapin. I vote for Richard's doing *Man of La Mancha* next spring."

The discussion went on for several days. I was still against a wall. *Man of La Mancha* had too few girls in the cast. *Streets of New York* was silly. *Brigadoon* dealt too much with romance for a cast who knew only sex. *West Side Story* required a full-time dance instructor, which we didn't have. *My Fair Lady* was too involved with characterization through dialect. *Gypsy* was anti-mother. *Seventeen* was racist. *Peter Pan* concerned itself with getting out rather than getting in. *Carousel* was dangerous for immature voices. *Simply Heavenly* was too 1940. *Green Pastures* was patronizing. *Porgy and Bess* would bring pickets to the opening. *Finian's Rainbow* I hated because of personal prejudices towards things Irish. *Guys and Dolls* was disrespectful to my favorite charity. *Sound of Music* had no boys in it, and Gilbert and Sullivan was too musically oriented for our needs.

The list went on and on. Time was running out. Bruce was frantic; preparations for a major musical had to begin that June for a May opening in 1969.

Two weeks later Dr. Robbins took eight aspirins and later collapsed from an attack of bleeding ulcers. He was forced to take a two-week vacation. During that time he rediscovered daytime radio talk shows. To his surprise he learned of the several international companies of *Fiddler on the Roof,* including a recent Japanese production. Because of his own Russian-Jewish background he had special identification with this script. The fact that the Japanese could have similar personal experiences lessened whatever reservations he might have had concerning a black company. I had dismissed the possibility and was surprised to learn that he had given it some thought. I asked, "Would you approve a production if I made the request?"

"Dick, I have to give it a lot more thought. At this time I am absolutely certain that our black and Puerto Rican community would never accept presentation of a script about Jews."

Walking through the halls of a special-service school is at best an upsetting experience. Every child seen in the hall during class time should be challenged, and those who are cutting escorted either to their classes or to the dean for discipline. It goes without saying that when a teacher has a free period, he doesn't wish to interrupt his own business by challenging any of the countless children who enjoy roaming the building, smoking in the stairwells or lying in wait for sex. Some teachers, however, are assigned hall patrol to correct this situation.

When a new teacher stepped out of a chaotic classroom and asked for my help in regaining control of his class, I looked in and recognized one of the groups I had in a large once-a-week General Music period. I couldn't recall their being hostile, so I agreed to help rescue the situation and maybe show off a bit. I was very proud of my class-control techniques.

I entered the room and was greeted with raucous shouts of, "Hello, Mr. Piro." The tone was intended to insult their assigned teacher. I was under no delusion that they were glad to see me.

In the first week of September I had greeted all classes, including this one, with, "My name is Mr. Piro." As I print my name in large block letters on the board, I continue with, "It is, you will notice, just plain 'Piro' with four letters. You all know lots of good four-letter words. Some begin with *f* and some with *s*, so I'm offering you one that begins with *p*. It is not Shapiro, although many of you will call me Shapiro because in Brooklyn and New York City it is a common name. By doing so you will be taking away my proud Sicilian heritage and giving me another proud heritage of being a Jew."

(At this point there was usually a gasp since "Jew" is a forbidden word in school when white adults are present. It was part of their vocabulary of insults. The children had long picked up the discomfort their teachers—ninety percent of whom were Jewish—felt with the word and in its rare use it was usually changed to a comfortable "Jewish.")

We then discussed the fact that since my family arrived in the United States from Italy a mere forty years ago and their families had been here for hundreds of years, these children in the class were much more "American" than I was.

Invariably half the class would get up at the bell, stand in front of the large printed "Piro" on the board, and singsong, "Good afternoon, Mr. Shapiro."

I stood in front of the class waiting for their attention, totally ignored in the din. My plan to show off my instant-control technique was not working. I picked up a chair and threw it down, making as much noise as possible. There was a hushed silence. I started to compliment them on their usual excellent behavior and intended to make the point that it would be a pity if they spoiled their good reputation for a new teacher.

A girl directly in front of me was laboriously reading aloud from her social-studies book. (One of the things the new teacher had asked before he lost control was that the class read a page for subsequent discussion. Irma was obeying his orders, to the letter.) I continued my address, a shade louder. She increased her volume proportionately. In a violent gesture of fury, I swept Irma's desk with my arm. Her notebook scattered over the front of the room. She leaped out of the chair and put up her fists demanding that I pick up her things. Before I could gain control of my own temper I screamed, "When I ask for attention I want *all* the attention and that means you!" She was breathing heavily, working herself up to a familiar teen-age hysteria. I ignored her entirely and continued the complimentary address to the class.

She interrupted. "You goin' to pick up my things? You better pick up my books."

We were both standing in front of the class. The new teacher had moved to safety at the back in order to avoid what looked like a fight. The class was silent, delighted to see a confrontation. They knew about Irma's temper. After a pause, Irma snorted twice and then shouted full voice, "Pick up my books, you white motherfuckin' Jew bastard!" The class gasped in glee that Irma had shot off her strongest bolt. It was immaterial to them who won this confrontation.

I waited for pedagogical inspiration. It came. I looked at Irma, and then back to the class. Quietly, almost pleading, I said, "You know, ladies and gentlemen, the tragedy here is that when Irma smiles she is one of the prettiest girls in this school." (Irma was much taller than her classmates, and had a serious complexion problem coupled with hair that had obviously been ruined with chemical attempts at beautification. Unattractiveness at this point in her life was a major cause for seeking attention through violence.) "No kidding. I'd walk a mile for an Irma smile."

In spite of her effort to remain angry she began to melt, but stopped with an explosive "Sheee-it!"

"I was really lucky last December because Irma smiled when she gave me a lovely Christmas card." (It wasn't true.)

All at once Irma gave up the fight and burst out in a radiant smile that truly, to my surprise, made her pretty.

"There you go! For a smile as gorgeous as that I would do anything. I consider it an honor to pick up your books, which I had no right to throw on the floor in the first place."

Putting on as gallant an air as possible, I reached down and gathered her things, helped by the children near her. Then, bending one knee, I presented them as a knight to his queen. For the rest of the year Irma made it a point to come by the music room to say hello.

After class, I typed a memo. "Dr. Robbins: We will be doing *Fiddler on the Roof* as our spring musical next season."

Without waiting for reply, Bruce went into action immediately. We chopped up the script and photographed each of the song texts, along with every picture we could find from souvenir booklets and record albums, for use on a slide projector. We then taped the recording of the show and were off and running. Our plan was to present the story and score as a music-appreciation lesson to all classes.

Our first and most important presentation was made in the seventh-grade chorus class. Many of these twelve- and thirteen-year-olds had formed the children's chorus of orphans and thieves in *Oliver!* Most were looking forward to being drama majors and had personal stakes in our script selection.

"Boys and girls, we have finally selected our next musical," I announced. "It's called *Fiddler on the Roof* and it is a story about Jews."

They froze. A deep, chilling, only-as-black-kids-can-do-it freeze. Duane, who was scheduled to play Motel, broke the silence.

"Mr. Piro, you said you didn't like *Fiddler on the Roof* when you took Irving to see it last year."

"You're absolutely right, Duane, but I've had second thoughts about it. I said that I didn't like *Fiddler*. But what I should have said was that I didn't like the way *Fiddler* was presented on Broadway. I won't change the show, I promise, but what I will do is to restore some of the values I think they lost on Broadway."

"But—"

"Let's hold the questions until we can get through the lesson, OK?"

They settled in their seats with postures clearly indicating they would listen out of personal respect for me, not because of any interest in the material. I began with the story of Tevye, the poor dairyman, and played recordings of each song in sequence, sketching in the plot. The class read the lyrics projected on a screen overhead. I waited for reactions.

Nothing. I was stunned. These were *my* kids. This was part of the family that had just spent six months enduring the production agonies of *Oliver!* It was simply because we were a family that negative reactions were not more vocal. Their silence said, "This is Jewish and we don't respond to Jewish things."

For years students had been easily influenced by my own enthusiasm for a project. The choruses had hated learning sixteenth-century madrigals, but my enthusiasm eventually earned an equal response, until the music was appreciated and enjoyed for itself. When I decided to remove these madrigals from the concert program, they screamed their displeasure. *Fiddler* had to grab these children with its own merits and not mine.

The lesson ended. The class left silently.

By Friday we had finished listening to the *Fiddler* recording. I drew the brilliant yellow music score from my briefcase and said, "Now we'll sing along with Dick. Let's everyone do all the parts of 'Tradition,' and later we'll split up into mammas and papas. OK?"

The first bar was disaster. Not a mouth opened. No child was willing to break the contract they had made regarding things Jewish. I had an idea.

"Hey, let's do something different with this number, since it will be sung while the cast are dancing."

"Dancing?" Duane spat out. "Who can dance off that kind of stuff?"

"Jews can, Duane, and you can too."

Duane leaped up and performed an Afro-dance movement while trying to sing the song in a mocking fashion. The class roared its approval. To keep up the class spirit, I feigned disapproval of Duane's interruption.

"Thank you, Reb Duane, for this illuminating example of Afro-Jewish dance. With your permission I'd like to continue with my brilliant idea."

"You may continue, Reb Dick." More laughter.

"So, instead of singing the song right away, let's just give a kind of foot-tapping accompaniment. Then when that gets going, I'll ask for finger-snapping, some clapping—and maybe by then you'll be inspired to sing."

That did it. The children who were not totally turned off (but feared group censorship) had the opportunity of responding physically without being seen. A quiet foot-tapping began and quickly swelled as the entire class took part. At the end, "Tradition" was being sung lustily by everyone. The raucous value was all wrong but the spirit was exhilarating.

The bell signaled the end of the class and the children groaned because the "fun" was over. They poured out of the music room into the hall singing at the top of their voices: "Who day and night must scramble for a living, feed a wife and children, say his daily prayers? And who has the right as master of the house to have the final word at home? The Papa!"

Bruce intercepted me on the way to the lunchroom. "What's going on?" he asked. "I thought you told me they hated it."

"Not any more, Bruce. I fear the fiddlers are going to fiddle throughout this building and then the shit is going to hit the fan. The anti-Semite is about to strike again."

The material had sold itself. I arranged each lesson so that by dismissal the excitement had built to a pitch where the children would go on to their next class singing. No objections were voiced by the community, but certain teachers went into shock. Bruce began to monitor faculty-lunchroom conversations in which some teachers said the children were singing the *Fiddler* music in "a most disrespectful manner."

These youngsters were no dopes. Once they caught on, they arranged to pass by those teachers' rooms for a moment's serenade from the *Fiddler* score.

We still lacked definite approval from Robbins, but felt there could be no objection to doing the score as a music-appreciation lesson in General Music.

Meanwhile, Robbins voiced several objections to *Fiddler,* chief of which was the anticipated negative reactions of the community when they learned we were "jamming Jewish culture down the kids' throats." This, coupled with the memory of the unsuccessful *Oliver!* boycott, kept him in a state of flux, so that he neither approved nor disapproved a production of *Fiddler.* I took this as a typically Robbins-style signal to go ahead. Bruce was disturbed by Robbins' indecision.

"If he's not really hot on the idea now," he said, "what's going to happen when the going gets tough?"

"The important thing to remember, Bruce, is that he didn't say no. He can pull out of this at any moment, but he's saying, 'Go ahead until I get more feedback from the staff.' That gives us more time to get our own shock troops in action. There is little love for the teachers who are going to oppose us on this from either the staff in general or the community. It may boil down to a confrontation. In an effort to spite these teachers the community just may demand *Fiddler on the Roof.*"

"You'd allow it to come to that?"

"I think this is the right show for the right kids at the right time. I am so convinced of this that I will utilize any and all help, even when it's given for the wrong reasons. I'll make some phone calls tonight and start the ball rolling in the other direction."

3

No director admits to precasting, but hardly a director exists who hasn't wished to produce *Hamlet* simply because he's discovered the ideal Hamlet. For two years, unknown to us, we had been grooming the perfect Golde and the near-perfect Tevye. Beginning in the sixth grade when they were members of my homeroom class, Teddy Smith and Beverly Cannon had benefited by diverse theater experiences. They had distinguished themselves as members of the *Oliver!* ensemble—especially Teddy, who, on a fifteen-minute notice, took over the feature role of Mr. Sowerberry on opening night and stopped the show. But, since a Tevye and a Golde by themselves do not a perfect *Fiddler* make, I was concerned about weaknesses in the secondary feature parts and overjoyed to discover that several of the following year's drama class had registered for my summer-school theater course at Junior High School 275. It augured well as an opportunity to develop and train these youngsters but, more important, it gave us a chance to get closer as human beings and experience the togetherness which makes perfect casting inevitable.

Thus my excitement about the proposed summer production of *Comedy of Errors* featuring the future *Fiddler* cast obliterated feelings of nostalgia at seeing the *Oliver!* season go into the yearbook as history. I was especially eager to work with children who attended class for no reason other than personal choice. Sharing this program with me would be Irving Williams, a former student who would function as an educational assistant. Irving was an outstanding graduate of Junior High School 275 and had taken leading roles in our productions of *Taming of the Shrew* and *Romeo and Juliet.*

To Irving I was "Mr. Cool," and to me he represented a seventeen-year-old middle-of-the-road nonmilitant black in a seething ghetto. He was vital as an individual who in his way reflected the values of what has become known as the "silent black majority." Along with the usual difficulties of a black teen-ager imprisoned in a ghetto he also showed a certainty of his potential as a useful human being capable of achieving his dreams. He worked hard at the appearance of ease but, drawn to excellence as a challenge, the closer he came, the more frightened he was of achievement.

As usual, Irving was waiting outside the auditorium doors when I arrived one hot July day. I threw him the keys and we set about opening shop for the improvisation class. He walked over to the master light switch.

"No, Irving, please," I cautioned. "Lights make heat."

He hesitated, nervously realizing that I'd probably expect to chat until the class arrived. My suggestion thus deprived him of an excuse to avert his eyes, which he feared would reflect his gladness in seeing me—a gladness not in keeping with his being "cool." Irving was generally successful in keeping his responses low-keyed; but occasionally his eyes would flash with a spontaneous reaction and he'd let go with, "Oh, jive, Mr. Piro!"

I sat down on the edge of the stage and removed the lid

from a container of coffee. Irving paused opposite me, ill at ease. "What's happening this morning?" he asked.

"Irving," I began, "yesterday I had a second meeting with a guy named Howard Enders. He's an independent film producer. He's good and rather well known. You're going to get a kick out of meeting him. He's like a mirror of you only in negative. I'm not referring to race."

"Is he colored?" Irving asked.

"No. He's white. Irv, you know I hate it when you say 'colored.' "

"I'm sorry, Mr. Piro. I meant to say 'black.' "

"Anyway," I continued, "where you're always trying to come on like cool, this guy Enders really works at being a boy and actually says things like 'golly' and 'gee whiz.' He's on fire with our ideas about *Fiddler* and wants to do a film about it. His thing is that he feels guilty about living so safe and comfortable in the suburbs with his wife, kids, and trees. He wants to get involved."

"I dig it, man."

"But there's a catch, and that may involve you—the real Irving Williams, who is still standing, dammit, and using up all this good coolness. For heaven's sake, Irv, sit down." Irving sat down and immediately bent over to tie his sneaker, avoiding my eyes.

"What do I have to do?" he asked.

"Well, Enders needs some specific examples of black anti-Semitism that will help him in selling the idea when he goes looking for funds."

While we were talking, the class started entering the auditorium, curious about the dimness. The summer program was barely a week old and most were still in awe of Irving and me. (I had given Irving an extended buildup at the first session.) They took front seats; thirteen frightened eleven- and twelve-year-olds in a room seating five hundred and ninety. Irving jumped off the stage, embarrassed to have the others see our intimacy.

The buzzer rang and the quiet conversations dribbled to silence. I looked over the group, and focused on Connie Brown, eleven, who was shyest of the group. As the buzzer sound died, I sensed the class's reaction to my wearing shorts, and said, "No, Connie, I do not shave my legs and that's why they're so hairy. I'm the only one here who has an Afro of the knees." She looked up and gasped at the sudden focus of attention. As the group relaxed, I flipped on the tape recorder.

"As you know, we're going to be doing *Fiddler on the Roof* as our next major musical. Diane, since you're a very bright and pretty and honest person—what is *Fiddler on the Roof* about?"

With mock humility, since she had already experienced the show through a music-appreciation lesson, she said softly, "It's about tradition."

"Good answer. What kind of people are in *Fiddler*?"

"They Jews, and always complaining."

"Diane, how many Jews do you come in contact with during the day?"

"Two."

"Do any of you kids, or even the adults, come into contact with more than two or three Jews a day?"

The heads indicated a negative response in spite of the fact that their current school staff, as well as that of their previous elementary schools, was at least ninety percent Jewish.

"Who can describe a Jew for me?" I asked. No answer. "Is there a Jew in this room?" Someone looked at Irving and giggled.

"No, I'm sorry. Irving just happens to have a Jewish name."

Irving sank lower into his seat. Obviously he had not yet learned to cope with the ridicule value of his first name. Just then Ronnie Whetstone stood up to his full four feet and moved from his seat to the edge of the stage. With one hand holding together his perpetually broken glasses, he reached for the microphone, and with a voice that belied his size said, "Well, what a Jew is, is a person who came from Israel and you know they came from Israel and they be treated as if they were the best people around."

After the murmurs of assent died down, I asked Diane if she agreed with Ronald.

"Yes," she said. "A Jew is a person which is better more than anybody else."

We opened a game of instant word association which began with the word "Jew." The children were familiar with this game as an acting exercise and their responses came fast: "Religion. Cheater. Chap. Nothing. Greedy. A person."

Through deductive questioning one attitude was emphasized. If a person was white and liked by the child it was out of the question that he could possibly be Jewish. On the contrary, any white that exhibited less than admirable attributes was automatically "condemned" as a Jew.

"Ronnie," I asked, "where does the Jew, meaning the group, stand in relation to black people?"

"Well, they come in our neighborhoods and they take up our stores and cheat all us little colored kids 'cause they think we don't know nothing and it happened to me one time 'cause there was this Jewish man and he worked in the store and now he's out because the Negro people reported him and if he would do that in the white community they wouldn't tolerate that in the first place. They'd make sure that wouldn't happen in their community!"

Each of the children reported having at least one Jewish friend for whom he was willing to dispense with the usual anti-Semitic accusations. The one Puerto Rican boy in the group, George, summed it up when he said, "I like the boy Jews but not the grown-up ones."

The interviews continued with these fifth- and sixth-graders with the same theme repeated over and over again. I marveled that these youngsters, so aware of drugs, sex, perversion, and food-shelter-survival, should be so totally ignorant of differences within the white group. "Jew" was something abstract—something bad and to be avoided for reasons they weren't sure of but nevertheless acted upon in specific ways. I thought, "At the end of *Fiddler* maybe they'll still distrust Jews, but at least they're going to have basic awareness of what a Jew is, and some insight into cultural similarities." I also wondered why kids who have been daily exposed to Jews from the age of five had been kept in ignorance of the ethnic-religious background of their teachers. Was it intentional? And if so, why?

The ninety-minute period ended. I thanked the class and they left. Irving and I were alone again. I saw him tighten up in anticipation of our proposed in-depth follow-up, so we began with simple biographical data. His parents were both from the deep South and had come to New York City as teenagers. Remembering the incident about his name, I asked, "Irving, as a black, you have obviously been ribbed most of your life for having a Jewish name. Does it bother you? Did it ever?"

"Yeah, it used to bother me," he answered, with his eyes looking inward to another time. He clenched his teeth and said, "I couldn't stand it. Just because of the way they say it. It's just when you small and somebody calls you a Jew you think it's something bad."

"Would you say there was any anti-Semitism in this community of Brownsville?"

"Oh, yes."

"How do you know?" I asked.

"From the people I hang out with. The people who I work with. The colored people who have gotten somewhere say that no white person will ever get my job or something like that. And I know they're talking mostly about Jews and don't like them that much because they're . . . I don't think they're that intelligent, anyway."

"Who?"

"The people around here."

"You mean the blacks or the Jews?"

"Both of 'em."

What I was looking for was approaching. Presenting an air of nonchalance I asked, "Would you say that people in this neighborhood, the blacks, tended to use the word 'white' when they mean 'Jewish' and the reverse—that 'white' and 'Jew' kind of mean the same thing?"

"Yeah. That's where it's at."

Time was running out and I was anxious to end the session before the next class arrived.

"Irving," I asked, "do you remember when we went to Broadway to see *Fiddler on the Roof*?"

"Yeah. It was a good show."

"Do you think it's a good idea to do it here?"

"Well, it seems like the Negro kids will like it but I don't know how the Jewish people are going to take it. I don't think they're going to like it."

"Why do you think the Negro kids will like it?"

"They're going to rib it, I think."

I moved away from Jews and towards Shakespeare by asking, "Irv, let's talk about the villain in *Romeo and Juliet*. You played Tybalt, right?"

Irving looked up sharply, about to contradict my use of the word "villain." I interrupted him. "You don't think of Tybalt as a villain?"

"No. Well, he did kill Mercutio, but . . . he wasn't that bad."

"When you played him didn't you feel mean and hateful?"

"At first I tried to but I didn't get anywhere. You kept screaming at me that you weren't convinced. Then I read over all of his scenes and no matter how hard I tried I still felt good about Tybalt. He did what he had to do. He wasn't bad. It was all an accident, just like Juliet's death was. But I guess people don't look at it that way."

"Do you get what I'm driving at about our *Fiddler*?"

"Yes. I think I do. The kids will probably become Jews the way I became Tybalt. You've got to love the character you're playing or else the play won't work."

"Exactly."

The buzzer rang for lunch. Before we could escape, the room started filling with some of the projected *Fiddler* players who had come to talk and jive while Irving and I ate our box lunches. The difference between the eleven- and twelve-year-olds at the morning session and these children was much greater than the year or so in age. Reggie, Teddy, Duane, Eileen, and Robin had all basked in the adulation surrounding *Oliver!* and were proud that they would be moving from the chorus into featured roles. They, unlike the younger ones, had no awe of the Piro presence. We had been intimately involved in two years of experiences including the Somerset, Massachusetts, exchange programs, visits to my Manhattan home, and several Broadway theater trips. They moved into the auditorium and took over, as I expected them to.

Starting a playback of the tape, I suggested that they might want to add their wisdom to that of the younger ones. *Fiddler* was their property and they listened closely. Midway through, more to foil Teddy's attempt to tease Eileen than to get information, I asked, "Teddy, in playing the possibilities of Tevye, give me some opinions. Like describe what a Jew is—not Tevye—but any Jew."

At a glance from me, Irving quickly placed a fresh reel on the machine. Teddy paused.

"What is a Jew, Teddy?"

"Well, really, I don't know. A Jew is a human being just like everybody else, as far as I know."

"Reginald, you're going to be playing Perchik, a sort of revolutionary Jew. Would you say Jews are prejudiced against blacks?"

"Some are and some are not. Some Negroes hate Jews and some Jews hate Negroes."

"Very liberal," I mocked. "What about the Jews that you know? Are they uncomfortable in your presence?"

"Most of my teachers are."

"That's not because you're black, bigmouth, it's because you're Reginald."

"Very funny, Mr. Piro."

"Thank you, Reginald. Let's get a girl in on this. Eileen, where do you think the blacks stand in relation to the Jews?"

"I don't know. I don't even understand your question."

"OK, good point. First of all, whose community is this?"

"Well, on one side of this school is the Negro community and on the other side is the Jewish community."

"On the other side of the school?" I asked. "You mean on the streets or an imaginary line somewhere?"

"An imaginary line."

"Is there much mixture between the two—Jews and blacks?"

"No, not that much, because now they have like housing problems with all the white people. They're moviing to the white people's section and then when another Negro person moves in the first Negro moves right back out again. But the areas become mostly Negro, anyway. That happened where I used to live."

"Well," I asked, innocently, "why would a person move out just because a Negro family moved in next door?"

"Some people just don't like Negroes, that's all. Some Negroes go around dropping stuff on the streets just like the Jews do but maybe the Jews don't like it."

I said, "Robin, why do you think a Jew would move out of a neighborhood if a Negro moved in?"

" 'Cause one black family moves in, two black families moves in. And then two more black families move in. Some Jews just can't stand black people. That's all there is to it." She sat down, satisfied with her explanation.

If Irving and I were to have lunch we had to get rid of this gang for at least an hour. I summed up with, "Does anyone have some final words for the world before we close this off?"

Eileen pugnaciously thrust herself into the center of the group.

"I want to ask somebody, anybody, something," she began. "How come when Jewish people dance they don't have no kind of rhythm?"

Squeals of laughter erupted from the children because of both the smart-alecky tone of Eileen's question and the fact that it was me she was baiting.

Reggie, laughing hardest, asked, "Hey, can I answer that?"

"Be my guest."

"Very interesting," he said with a thick German accent, "but very stupid."

Robin jumped up and added, "Hey, Mr. Piro, that's probably what the Jews think—why the Negro dancers have no rhythm."

Eileen pushed Robin aside and grabbed for the microphone.

"What are you saying, Robin? We got a lot of rhythm. We got *enough*."

I implored the group to leave us so that we could have lunch in peace. We finished, and I went to the general office. Standing at the mailboxes was William Johnson, a black who held the title of District Human Relations Coordinator. Some teachers had dubbed him the District Superintendent's token Negro, and, in spite of whatever ideas he held on the subject of race relations, his primary function was to "yes" his boss into thinking they were both doing the job. Other schools in the district were about to go under with racial violence. Ours was quiet. Under the leadership of Assistant Principal Mrs. Amelia Brown, we had used all our resources to get the people in the community together to solve common problems. Why the Human Relations Coordinator was assigned for the summer to our particular school was a good question no one asked.

I related the morning's experience to Mr. Johnson. He expressed regret at not being present at the actual interviews. I asked Irving to set up a machine in the office and started a tape playback. The secretaries gathered around, pleased to have a break in their routine, and Irving and I returned to the auditorium to greet the incoming cast for a rehearsal of the summer production of *Comedy of Errors*. We left the tape running to the delight of the white office staff and Mr. Johnson.

In the auditorium the group assembled, heard suggestions about the previous day's rehearsal, and were ready to go on stage without their leading lady—Eileen. Suddenly there was a frantic pounding on the door. Irving went to open it. Eileen burst in and ran down the aisle shouting, "Mr. Piro! Mr. Piro! They're playing our *tape* in the general office right *now!*"

"I know that, Eileen," I said calmly. "Who do you think gave it to them and set up the equipment? What's the problem?"

She looked up with a combination of fear, panic, and anger. "But Mr. Piro, they's *white* people listening!"

She froze with her mouth open, staring at me. Then, without another word, she made a grand entrance onto the stage and assumed her opening position for *Comedy of Errors*. We were familiar with Eileen's volatile nature, and none of us dared laugh. But as the youngsters glanced at one another, the auditorium came alive with silent mirth.

4

On Sunday, September 9, the rank and file of the United Federation of Teachers voted to strike. Two days later we voted to return to school but gave Union executives power to call another work stoppage after giving a forty-eight-hour notice. Agreements were not met. We were called out on Friday the thirteenth and remained on strike until September 30. Upon returning to work, inspection teams representing both sides of the dispute were sent to the troubled schools to verify charges. We worked for two nervous weeks; then another general strike vote was taken. This time it lasted nearly two months.

On Sunday, October 15, I placed my ballot to strike in the box and made a mental note to call up the key drama kids and get them to my apartment for rehearsal the next morning. A choice might have to be made. If this strike continued as long as threatened, it might not be possible to get two major productions—*The Crucible* and *Fiddler on the Roof*—out of the cast. At that time we were about finished with *Crucible* until we could get on a stage and start blocking scenes. I decided to take the gang uptown to the Drama Book Shop the next afternoon and buy *Fiddler* scripts. We would pass by the Broadway theater where it was playing and look at the photographs. It would be a good trip.

As I rounded Seventh Avenue to enter my building at Sixteenth Street, I inadvertently bumped into a couple. I looked up to apologize. It was Mitchell Grossman, the English teacher who had led the *Oliver!* boycott the year before.

"Hi, Mitch! I was so engrossed in plans for . . . Hey, isn't this exciting?"

He was taken aback and obviously embarrassed. I filled the silence. "And why haven't I seen you on the walk to school lately?"

"Because I got married and moved. This is my wife."

"Hey, that's more exciting than the strike."

He introduced us. Here was a chance to mend fences.

"What the hell are we standing on the sidewalk for," I interrupted, "when I live eleven flights up? Why don't you go vote and then drop in for coffee?"

Mitch was silent. His wife said, "Thanks, Dick, we'd really like that but we're with some other people. They're parking the car. We really have to get back to Brooklyn. The dog and all that crap, you know. Can we take a rain check and make it another time?"

"Sure. See you at the war's end."

Long ago I had decided that the only basis for a relationship with Mitch Grossman consisted of discussing theater while we walked to and from the train. He was in touch with the New York scene and his opinions were interesting. We always seemed to avoid discussions of school and the kids. He did not impress me as a teacher.

Two years earlier, during my first year in Brooklyn, I took a day off from personal teaching assignments and followed my homeroom to all of their classes. The purpose was to investigate their functioning in academic situations as well as to satisfy my own curiosity about the quality of their teachers.

This was a difficult eighth grade. All had exceptionally low reading scores. With the exception of myself and Steve Kaplan, then their art instructor, most teachers dreaded their period with class 8-16. I was particularly interested in their English-class performance since ability to do this subject could help them achieve in the rest of their school work.

Mitch presented a lesson on grammar which indicated preparation on his part. However, at no point did he *teach* a lesson, since the children refused to focus on any one thing at any one time—not on Mitch, not on me in the back of the room, not on the blackboard, and not on the text in front of them. The terrible echo acoustics of the room added to the din. This was not an unusual situation in a school such as ours. What shocked me was that Mitch either did not notice the lack of attention or else—worse—didn't care. He went on with his lesson oblivious to all but two listening children. Afterwards we spoke about some of the kids, but never about the teaching. My sympathy was with the children. He gave them no reason to forsake their business for his.

A year passed before I had another experience with him as a teacher. Several times a week certain drama students cut his English class and asked if they could remain with me for the period. As a professional it was my duty to discipline them. Cutting any class was forbidden. I shirked the responsibility. It was either that or have them roam the halls and get into more serious trouble than a simple act of cutting class. They joined whatever class I had. If I were free we would have a bull session backstage or else work on costumes and scenery. Eventually a pattern was set: when these boys were scheduled for English they stayed with me.

"How do you expect to pass English if you never attend the class?" I asked Jon.

"Mr. Grossman doesn't care. He'll pass us anyway, just to get rid of us."

"Come on now, Jon, no teacher 'doesn't care' if a kid consistently cuts his class. I'd be furious."

"No, Mr. Piro. He always asks us if you have anything for us to do. So we tell him yes and he lets us go."

"In other words, Jon, you're using me to get out of his class, right?"

"Right."

"I resent that. If you haven't the balls to simply cut Grossman's class then you don't deserve to be with me. He can flunk you, you know, and blame me."

"Look, Mr. Piro, he hates us anyway, so what's the big deal?"

I doubted their conclusions, being fully experienced with the children's attempts to play one teacher against another. However, I found it odd that an English teacher would want to get rid of kids with excellent reading abilities, all of whom had been turned on to theater through involvement with Shakespeare, and, most recently, Charles Dickens. I also found it strange that, even if he thought I wanted these children for extra sessions, he never mentioned it. In the rare occasions when I needed to pull children out of academic class, I expected righteous indignation from teachers. The evidence was stacking against Mitchell.

With these thoughts I got off the elevator, entered my apartment, and phoned Teddy, my star; Beverly, his leading lady; and Mary, Duane, and Reggie, secondary leads.

"Listen to the eleven-o'clock news. If it looks like a strike—which it does already—call the other kids and be at my apartment tomorrow by ten. If you can't use your bus passes, then do your flying-wedge business and we'll plan another legal system."

Entrance to a subway never presented problems to these children. If they lacked the fare they waited until several people were lined up to buy tokens. Then they formed a flying wedge and rushed through the pass gate, fully aware that the token attendant was not permitted to leave his booth. Once on the other side, they separated and ran to different locations. At best a transit cop could catch only one. It was an old New York City game.

The next morning at nine o'clock the doorbell jarred me awake. I had overslept, having been up late the night before celebrating the victorious strike vote. My apartment was a studio with no bedroom. I shouted, "Just a minute," and frantically threw the sofa bed together. I padded to the door in a robe. It was Jana Myers, one of the uncast mammas of *Fiddler,* with her little brother Alvin, whom I had not met since he was still in elementary school, and a neighbor's child Jana was entrusted to mind during the day. We were all flustered. I dressed while Jana found WWRL, the soul-music station, and then excused myself to go to the supermarket for the lunch food I had promised the group. I returned laden with packages of potato chips, sodas, pickles, candy bars, ice cream, and the makings of English-muffin pizzas. A few minutes later the bell rang again.

Lining both legs of the L-shaped hall were about twenty fourteen- and fifteen-year-olds. Led by Teddy Smith, they marched down each hall, crisscrossed, and entered my door singing "Consider Yourself At Home" from *Oliver!*. They paraded around the living room and back out, and as the number concluded they formed the same tableau we had performed at school. They collapsed in laughter. It was a brilliant opening for the longest teacher strike in educational history.

I might as well not have been there and it was exactly as I wanted it to be. They took over the house. Duane sat at my desk and carefully went through it, drawer by drawer, in idle curiosity. He discovered a packet of cigarette papers. I held my breath waiting for a Does-Mr.-Piro-smoke-pot routine, but instead he caught my eye, winked, and then placed the packet neatly behind some books. The moment was private between us. Some children were dancing, others arguing about the next day's meeting procedures, and the rest exploring the other areas: bathroom, kitchenette, and closets. I knew Jana had brought some strangers but I was curious about the two boys sitting politely in a corner. I began questioning them and one boy replied, "We saw the kids getting on the train and asked where they were all going. They said to your house so we decided to come along." I welcomed them and explained that my house was very small so subsequent days had to be limited to cast members only. They understood. The few graduates present, who knew they were always welcome, had decided to get in on the action. I knew some schools had been opened for the duration of the strike by black teachers. They were offering remedial work in small-class situations. I suggested these graduates ease into their new high schools by attending the "freedom schools."

I got up and turned off the radio.

"Everybody into the living room," I called. "We're going to work on *The Crucible*. Duane?"

"What?"

"Would you get the chair in the kitchen and place it beside the sofa. Tina?"

"Oh lordy!"

"You lay—lie?—down on the sofa. Duane, you'll kneel on the floor beside Tina. The audience will be over here. Move when and if you feel like it. Then—"

Duane asked, "How am I going to know when to move?"

"Good point, Duane. First of all don't bother with the stage directions in the script. They're written in italics. Move if you must and—"

"I still don't understand, Mr. Piro."

"I want you to get the feel of each other. Duane, there are times you want to be right next to someone and times you'd rather not, right? Sometimes you can't explain why but it just seems right. Do that. Just let your feelings direct your body. It's complicated sounding but you'll get the hang of it right away. Everybody ready?"

The remaining children cleared a playing area and I moved over to the phonograph to monitor the opening music. Lolita, playing Tituba, the Barbados slave, came out of the bathroom and crept up to the sofa. She leaned over Duane, looked at Tina and said, "Me Betty be hearty soon?"

The room erupted in laughter, including mine.

"Lolita, that's incredible! Where did you learn the West Indian accent? My God, you sound so there!"

Lolita was very pleased with herself. She was seriously overweight and never relaxed because of constant cast teasing. She walked to a chair, sat down, and crossed her legs to lengthen her moment. Then very humbly said, "I went over to our West Indian neighbors and just listened to them talk. I didn't expect it to be so funny."

"You do know why we laughed, Lolita? We laughed because the perfection of the accent knocked us out. I mean we expected to hear a little bit of Brooklyn Lolita but then out came Tituba all the way. Wow! OK, let's go on. We've just spent ten minutes over one line."

Duane and Tina resumed their positions. Duane clasped his hands in traditional prayer fashion.

"What are you doing, Duane?"

"I'm prayin'."

"Why? Are you in church?"

"No."

"Where are you, Duane?"

"In Betty's bedroom."

"Who is Betty?"

"My daughter."

". . . who was discovered dancing naked in the forest by you, her father. She fainted. She's still out and you're scared."

Duane was attentive but not listening. "OK," I said, "Duane, stand up behind the chair. Look at Tina. Really look at her and study her eyes, her hair, her nose. Now think of the things I said. See the situation that happened last night. Feel those same feelings—shock, disgust, fear. This is your little girl. She's innocent. Who did this terrible thing to her? What will happen to you when the town finds out? But she may be sick or even dying. What about evil spirits and witches? Now, what is the thing you most want to happen?"

Silence.

"Come on," I pleaded. "What is it you most want to do?"

"Fuck!" he yelled. The room exploded. Before I could respond the door opened. It was Dan O'Neil, creative writing teacher, accompanied by five of his student reporters. They had come to cover the rehearsal. They no sooner found places on the floor when the bell rang again.

"Goddammit," I snorted. "Teddy, please see who it is."

He went to the door and returned.

"Mr. Piro, you're not going to believe this. There's a lady, a little girl, and a basket of kittens."

Some of the girls screamed. They hated cats. I remembered answering an ad in the *Village Voice* for free delivered kittens. I went to the door and welcomed the lady and her daughter. They seemed frightened. They quickly spread the kittens around the floor and we selected the most assertive male. The woman gathered up the rest and fled with her daughter. The argument as to what to name the newest member of the cast ended in a stalemate. Thus he was forever dubbed Puss.

That over, I tried once again to get the rehearsal moving.

"Duane, I'm really surprised. Last summer you spent two months rehearsing *Comedy of Errors* with me and you were the best Dromio I have ever seen. What are you playing in *Fiddler*?"

"Motel the tailor."

"Now I ask you to shift into the same theater bag and all you can think about is fucking Tina?"

"Well, Mr. Piro, what would you think if you were standing over a girl who is laying on a big sofa with her eyes closed?"

Tina shifted position and looked intently over the rims of her huge glasses. She was getting ready for a defense.

"If I were a fourteen-year-old boy," I continued, "with my brains between my legs, Duane, I might possibly think of sex, but if I were a fourteen-year-old talented actor with a record of several fine performances, I might think of the play. You're her *father!*"

"So?" Tina said. "There's a girl on my block that . . ."

"I don't want to hear it, Tina. Let's go on for just one half hour. The girls that aren't in the scene can go into the kitchen and start lunch. I'm not going to do the impossible. The excitement about the strike seems to be too much for the seriousness of this play. Frankly, I don't feel much like working, either. After lunch we're all going uptown to buy scripts of *Fiddler on the Roof*. But until then, will you give me just thirty minutes of concentration?"

"Come on, let's do it," urged the other children.

I liked the spirit of this group and was unwilling, at that time, to stifle it with work. We had unlimited time. It was best to let personal chemistry work its way.

When the first batch of pizzas was ready, I showed the group the location of the trays, silverware, napkins, and some small folding chairs. They opened the drop-leaf table and spread out the food. Some had brought their own sodas and began bargaining with the others over the selection of flavors I had bought. Eventually everyone settled in a spot with paper plate, plastic cup, and food. I noticed Eileen's plate was empty.

"Hey, Eileen, aren't you eating or are you being polite?"

This was her cue. She stood up and adjusted her African turban (her mother would not permit her to wear a full Afro hairdo) and slowly walked to the closet. She was enjoying her moment of stage attention. Duane caught my eye and we winked at each other. Eileen was just under five feet tall and perfectly proportioned in sensuous womanly flesh. Her sharp features glowed a dark walnut, clear and scrubbed. She was fully aware of her beauty.

From her purse she drew out a small paper bag while humming a tuneless rhythm. "I brought my own, if *you* don't mind," she said, in her best high-pitched, husky Butterfly McQueen, voice. I took the bag and opened it. One raw pork chop wrapped in foil. The group waited and watched. I looked at Eileen. She was smiling and daring me to make a racial slur.

"Do you have something I can cook it on, Mr. Piro?"

"If you brought your own food, Eileen, I should think you would have brought something to cook it with plus, maybe, a little salt and pepper? I mean, if you're going to do your thing, why not do all of your thing—you know, chitlins, ham hocks, greens, co'n braid . . ."

The tension broke and the children laughed. Eileen was again presenting her hostile image: "I don't want nothin' from no white man." It was her game and everyone, including the children, knew it. They enjoyed her confrontations as theater.

With no further remarks—and it wasn't easy—I steered her in the right direction and she cooked her pork chop. The rest ate their fill and, unaware that I was watching, stuffed their pockets. On order, the boys gathered trash together. There was argument as to who would run the vacuum cleaner. With the place as clean as it was upon their arrival, I suggested we take a long break and go script buying. My plan was to walk around Greenwich Village and then go uptown.

We headed down Seventh Avenue, crossed Greenwich Avenue, and then walked the length of Eighth Street to St. Marks Place singing *Oliver!* songs. At the first delicatessen, Beverly, Mary, Sharon, and Tina went in to discover pure gold—old deli-pickles. Since, as they informed me, Brooklyn delicatessens carried only new deli-pickles, this was indeed a find. (I was to spend the rest of the school year buying and delivering pickles to the girls on consignment.)

Although Brownsville is only a forty-five-minute subway ride from Greenwich Village, it represented to the children a sort of mythical never-never land. Here people were really free to wear and act and say what they wanted. They marveled at styles in shop windows and aped each person wearing outrageously long hair, a short miniskirt, or a transparent blouse. No one mentioned it in my hearing, but each of the several interracial couples we passed was noted and, I learned later, reserved for further private discussion on the train ride home. As usual, transvestites, especially the black ones, brought the strongest reactions.

At Cooper Square we halted at the outdoor sculpture there —a gigantic black metal cube balanced on one corner. It is attached to a swivel base which allows passers-by to turn it with little effort. Perched atop the cube was one of the then-rare flower-power hippies. Obviously on a happy trip, he was grooving on a bunch of wilted flowers clutched to his bosom. The youngsters fanned out, observing. He noticed us at once and opened his arms, letting the flowers drop to his lap.

"Hello, all my black brothers and sisters. I love you. I'm white and I'm sorry."

Too stoned to go on, he started throwing flowers one by one. The children scrambled to catch them. Duane and Ronald discovered the cube's mobility and, with a signal to Anthony, they began making it revolve. The flower child enjoyed this new trip and urged them to "make further contact —reach out and turn the world on its axis of love and brotherhood." The girls joined the boys and began pushing the sculpture faster. After several revolutions the hippie screamed, "Please. Please stop! I'm dizzy. Please. I have no more flowers. I love you."

In silent agreement they pushed faster and faster. The hippie gracefully slid off his perch and reached out to embrace Duane who immediately scrambled to the top of the cube. The game resumed with Duane saying, "Hello, all you black mothers. I hate you. I'm black and proud." He too was dethroned and replaced by another youngster. A crowd gathered to be entertained by a group sing of *Oliver!* songs followed by a medley of *Fiddler* melodies sung with nonsense words.

We roamed around St. Marks Place and then headed for the train since it was getting on toward three o'clock. I had promised their mothers I would get them home before four. We took the train up to Fiftieth Street. Although most had passes, they insisted on showing me the flying-wedge routine. I refused to walk with them. As they crashed through the pass gate, the black attendant smiled indulgently. He turned to me and said softly, "They had good teachers."

Once inside the Drama Book Shop, the children stood in awe.

"Mr. Piro, everything here has something to do with dramatics? There must be a million plays on one wall, alone."

They spread through the shop. I purchased the *Fiddler* scripts and to the amusement of the clerks, handed each child a copy. Appointments were set for small groups for the remainder of the week. We did another flying wedge, and I left them in the subway at Fourteenth Street where I got off to go home. They continued on to Brooklyn.

That evening I felt warm and at ease with the world. I had the strike, the almost-vacation (being with kids under these circumstances could hardly be called working, I thought at the time). I smelled success with this bunch and couldn't wait to attack the guts of *Fiddler.* Two telephone calls altered the realities. The first was from my landlord.

"Mr. Piro, I understand that you had a number of children in your apartment today?"

"That's right."

"What's going on?"

"You know I'm a teacher and I'm on strike. I plan on meeting some of my children here. Usually there won't be that many. Today was sort of special, being the first."

"Well, that's very dedicated of you but you're going to have to meet them somewhere else. This is an apartment building, not a school."

"What's your problem, Mr. Winthrop?"

"Well, I've had several tenant complaints, and . . ."

"Complaints?"

"Yes. They complained that children were running around—"

"That is ridiculous! They came up the elevator and came into my apartment. When they left I was with them and we went outside immediately. They never 'ran' around the building."

"Mr. Piro, I can't have fifty black—"

"So that's where it's at! It's OK to have children visit you but *black* children are out?"

"That's not what I meant," he retreated.

I got very angry and screamed threats of racism, Urban League, Black Panthers, and the mayor's Commission on Human Rights. We both calmed down but left nothing solved. I was determined to warn the children that their behavior entering and leaving the building was of prime importance if we were to continue this project.

The second call was from a mother of one of my afternoon guests. She was furious.

"Mr. Piro, if your apartment needs cleaning I suggest that you go to an agency and hire help. I can hardly afford to send my son all the way into Manhattan so that he can *clean your house*. I'm not raising my boy to be no white man's cleaning woman!"

It was the mother of the boy who had fought hardest for the privilege of using the vacuum cleaner. I explained that the children were coming every day and though I was more than willing to go through the personal expense of feeding them, I certainly did not intend to spend the rest of my day cleaning up afterwards. I would be a dietitian but not a custodian. Part of the whole wonderful family feeling we were building was engendered through activities such as cleaning up afterwards.

She was very embarrassed and apologized.

"I asked Michael about his day and when he said, 'Then we cleaned up Mr. Piro's apartment,' I called you." We became good friends and eventually I was invited to her home for a dinner.

Two weeks of mutual therapy followed. Children were prompt at rehearsals as we alternated between small groups and company call. At the end of the first week, when all negotiations for ending the strike failed, we decided to throw our full resources into *Fiddler* and postpone *The Crucible* for another time. Those most disappointed were the leads of *Crucible* who were secondary in *Fiddler*. We were "together" in the black sense of the word, which meant mind meeting on various levels and being totally content to exist in each other's proximity. Rather than pre-plan lunch, I waited for the group to assemble and then asked, "Who feels like cooking today?"

"Hey, I can make a great tuna salad," screamed Iris.

"That why you always stink of onions, firemouth?" countered Duane.

"OK, Iris," I said, "take some boys and go buy the makings for thirteen; and no kissing in the supermarket, y'hear?"

She put one hand out for the money and the other on her hip and said, "Who wants to kiss flabby-lips Duane, anyway?"

"You do, Iris flat-nose, and don't lie." Duane chuckled.

"Your mind's always in the gutter, boy."

"That's right, gal, cause I got sheets and pillows in my gutter. Want to see?" He made as if to unfasten his belt.

"Get off of me, Duane!" Duane grabbed for Iris, but she was out the door laughing.

"Hey, remember," I warned, "no jiving in the halls. Remember the landlord. The hall is off limits for noise."

"Don't worry, Mr. Piro, we know," Iris promised.

Toward the beginning of the third week, the thrill of cleaning passed. They were perfectly content to leave the apartment without picking up. As the novelty of being in a teacher's home wore off they began to treat it more and more like a public building, which meant litter and some accidental destruction through rough play. This angered me. At school I could never accept our new building being turned into a slum with children urinating and defecating on stairwells, pulling down student art work from the bulletin boards, and scattering fruit peelings wherever they wished. My outbursts—"This is my school and where I live for seven hours a day. Why do you treat it like a garbage dump?"—always brought vacant stares. I encountered similar attitudes in my home and never understood the change in conditioning. As soon as a location became "theirs"—municipal—it ceased to command minimum respect. It became necessary to remind them constantly of the difference between what was theirs (their own homes), ours (the school), and mine (my apartment).

Some incidents necessitated asking a child to leave because of misbehavior. "If you are unable to concentrate you're disrupting the rehearsal. Thank you very much. We'll see you tomorrow."

In public school a teacher cannot legally force a student to leave the building. It can happen, but only after weeks of red tape, and the act is ultimately called "suspension." But to be constantly annoyed by a child who is not ready or willing to be serious, and then to be able to rise to your full height, point to the door, and growl, "Get out," is an experience every teacher should have once before retirement.

After three weeks I started receiving phone calls from cast mothers. They expressed financial difficulties in sending their children to Manhattan every day, what with carfare, lunch money, and new clothes. The first two took me by surprise. I agreed with them, sympathized with the problem, and ached to get my hands on their daughters. The third and fourth mothers got the truth. From the beginning the children had used bus passes for free transportation. In this the Transit Authority was cooperative. I provided food and drink and they returned home again via bus passes. However, some of the girls were asking for and getting money from their parents for transportation and lunch. This money was spent on old deli-pickles, french fries for the trip home, magazines, and cosmetics. I waited for the next company call and confronted the group with their dishonesty. They shrugged. Their attitude was, "Well, wasn't it grand while it lasted?"

I was a coward and refused to face the facts. They had been stealing from their mothers, knew it, and felt not the least bit of shame. They had, in effect, stolen from me. Their system dictated exploitation when and where it was possible. In their view they hadn't done anything wrong. The situation was painful and I dismissed it.

Contrary to my expectations, Teddy Smith, the "star" of the company, faithfully came to every rehearsal and made tremendous strides in the role of Tevye, the Jewish dairy farmer. Beverly was a perfect Golde with no problems beyond her loving rejections of Teddy's amorous advances. He was still very much an early adolescent, complete with no voice change or other physical marks of puberty, while Beverly was on the brink of womanhood—at times I suspected she had passed beyond it. She was tall with a carriage of natural elegance, consistently groomed to perfection, perceptive, informed, humorous, and understanding.

We had progressed as far as we could on lines. It was time to start learning music. With my friend Joe's permission, I moved the group down the block to his apartment, where he had a piano. This new scene also began as a novelty since Joe was a "real" professional actor. Though the children had met him several times, they were initially ill at ease in his tiny apartment. I opened his door and as usual he was on the phone. He paused long enough to say "Hello" and "Welcome" and then excused himself. We settled on the few chairs and the floor. Olga, our Yente, quietly asked, "Mr. Piro, is *Fiddler on theRoof* a popular show?"

"What, Olga?"

"I mean, do lots of people know about it?"

"Well the ad in the papers reads 'America's most acclaimed musical' and it's been running for five years on Broadway. So it's safe to assume that it is a popular show. Why?"

"Well, my mother didn't see it yet but she read the script and said that it sounded familiar to her—the story, I mean."

"That could be. Most of the script comes from Sholom Aleichem's *Tevye the Milkman* which many of us had to read sometime in school. Did your mother like it?" I turned to the rest of the group and added, "Have any of you gotten any feedback from home?"

"Any whatback?" Teddy asked.

"Feedback. I mean questions or opinions from other people."

"My mother asked me what you said about it," Beverly noted.

"What do you mean, 'what I said about it'?"

"I mean about our time. You know. About what it means."

"I still don't understand, Bev. You read the script so you know what it means. You're the leading lady. Why didn't you tell her the story?"

"Mr. Piro, you playin' with me?"

"Beverly, I'm serious. I don't understand you."

"My mother asked me if there was anything special in *Fiddler on the Roof* that could apply to our lives today, all right? You knew all along what I meant."

"You're right," I said, smiling. "And you are much too smart to let me get away with it. And you're also too lazy to do your own thinking. I resent having to think for you."

"Look who's talkin'."

"Beverly, did your mother really ask you that question?"

"No."

"Who did, then?" Pause. "Come on, Bev, it's me, remember?"

"Mr. Prager, my social studies teacher."

"What did you tell him? I suspect you want me to confirm that you said the right thing."

"Mr. Piro, I . . ."

"Beverly?"

"I told him you didn't bother about all that crap."

I groaned.

"Well, when I said that I didn't know he asked me why you didn't tell us."

"What did you say then?"

"I said you were a director and we were actors and we didn't have time to talk about the show because we was too busy doin' it."

"A very good answer that makes me look very bad."

Duane, always sensitive to my shifts in mood, asked, "What do you mean about looking bad?"

"I mean lots of people are going to be asking you lots of questions about the meaning of *Fiddler on the Roof* for now, today. And they expect me to preach to you about it."

"What's that got to do with—"

"And," I continued, "I'm not going to tell you. I will not waste time lecturing about meanings of this show outside of the basic script values. We're 1902 Jews looking forward, not 1969 Jews looking back."

Only Beverly, Olga, Mary, and Sharon had continued listening. Duane sensed some intellectualizing and tuned out, concentrating on Joe's oil paintings. Reggie was in a far corner.

"Reginald," I shouted. "Get your finger off of Sheila's pickle and answer a question."

"What question?"

"When you simmer down, I'll ask."

"I never was boiling, so ask, already."

"Three weeks in a play and already he's talking Jewish," Olga mimicked. The group focused on this new action.

"Reginald," I continued, aware of the attention, "who is Perchik?"

"He's a character in *Fiddler on the Roof*."

"What a brilliant, informative answer. For someone who is in the show and *playing* Perchik, that's very good. I mean, to notice all of that about him. Next time we have drama remind me to ask you if there isn't something Mr. Grossman has for you to do."

Reggie became angry. He reached up to stroke the scar on his forehead ("A gift from my father when I was a baby"). He was tall and thin, with a high forehead and short hair. His eyes were an opening to his whole personality—warm, believing, and very vulnerable. He worked hard to maintain position in the group.

"Tell us about Perchik, Reg."

"Well, he's from Kiev. He was a student in the university there. He comes to Anatevka and gets a job teaching Tevye's five daughters. His pay is only free food and a bed. Then he goes to Moscow, I think, but gets caught and goes to jail. No. Siberia. I guess it's the same thing. Hodel goes with him and they get married, I think."

"Reggie, why'd they send him to Siberia?"

"I don't really know. Something to do with politics?"

"Haven't you been even a little bit curious? I mean does it have anything to do with your preparation for the role?"

"Not yet. I mean, I haven't even learned all the lines that are in the script. Why should I bother with the other stuff?"

I asked the group, "I wonder if any one of the 'actors' in this room can answer that."

Teddy blurted out, "How can you start to act unless you know who the character is, Reginald?" Joe and I had been working privately with Teddy on just this thing—character preparation.

" 'If that character is going to inhabit your skin,' " Teddy quoted Joe, " 'then you've got to know how he thinks, how he feels, how he sees, and how he has sex.' "

Reginald did not like Teddy's authoritarian air and suspected foul play at his expense.

"How the hell am I supposed to find out? Mr. Piro, have you ever told me anything about Perchik that's not already in the script?"

"No, I haven't, Reginald," I said, pleased with the exchange and grateful to Teddy.

"Who's running Russia at the time of *Fiddler,* Reg?"

"I guess it was the Czar."

"What is a Czar?"

"The properly elected head of the government," he quoted from a source he hoped was valid.

"Elected?"

"Yeah. No. He's like a king or something. Only more. An emperor?"

"Something like that." Sheila giggled.

"Stop playing, Sheila," Teddy commanded.

I stopped the argument with, "Reginald, if the Czar was ruling Russia, how did the communists manage to get control?"

"Oh, that's easy. They had a revolution."

"Who made that revolution, Reggie?"

"The people. People like you and me. Ordinary people."

He jerked erect and glanced around, defensive yet proud. One hand scratched the scar. He had inadvertently quoted a line from the show. The group responded with praise. They were involved now and anxious for me to go on.

"Reginald, do you have any experience with revolution?"

"Mr. Piro, that's a stupid question. Of course not. I'm only fourteen."

"Do you know any revolutionaries?"

"Yeah. My uncle used to be a Minuteman but he got shot in 1776 because . . ."

"OK, smartass, do you know anything about black power?"

"Sure. Power to the people and the Black Panthers and all that other shit."

"It's not shit," screamed Eileen. "You'll see, Reginald Barrett, one of these days. You'll see."

"Reginald," I moved in for the point, "what would happen if a white guy came in here right now and started beating on you black kids and I was a Black Panther?"

"You'd beat the shit out of that white mother." The group loudly agreed.

"What did Perchik do at Tzeitel's wedding when the Russians came in to mess up the reception?"

"He attacked them and got hit on the head."

"Hey!" Duane exhaled gently. "I see what you mean, Mr. Piro. Reginald—I mean Perchik—is a sort of Jewish Black Panther of that time and he—"

The end of Duane's thought wasn't heard over the din of the others in their anxiety to have their own conclusions heard. From the corner I heard Tina shout to Anthony, "Mr. Piro certainly did not say that the Black Panthers were communists."

When I had their attention I asked, "Are there any lessons for 1969 in our play?"

"You bet your black ass there is," said Reggie, taking responsibility for this revelation.

"OK. Now that I did Reggie's thinking for him, I'm warning you. Lots of people are going to be asking you questions like this. I picked Reggie to do myself because his character of Perchik is the most obvious. Some of you are going to have more trouble finding 1969 meanings in 1902 characters. I want each of you to come up with something similar to what we did to Reggie. Beverly!" She jumped to attention.

"What?"

"Who is Golde?"

"Lady Bird Johnson."

That ended the discussion. When we recovered, Joe had hung up the phone in frustration and was ready to work.

"Gang, you all know my best friend? Well, he's 'Joe' to me and 'Mr. Sicari' for those who are uptight about calling a friend of mine 'Joe.' "

"Hi, Joe!" from everyone for the first and last time. When they referred to him they said 'Joe,' but they studiously avoided any direct address which would have necessitated a "Mr. Sicari." Joe moved to the piano.

"Dick asked me to give some suggestions and—" Squeals of laughter from everyone. Joe looked puzzled. I stepped in.

"All right, gang, pull yourselves together. We have work to do and I don't want to waste a minute of Joe's time. You may as well know that some of my older friends refer to me as 'Dick,' which is the common nickname for 'Richard.' It's the same thing with Robert-Bob, Elizabeth-Betty, Margaret-Peggy. If 'Dick' means something else in your charming subculture then you're just going to have to get used to it. So, when Joe says 'Dick' he's referring to my *name*."

It took twenty minutes to get them back to working order, especially the girls, who were faster at catching puns.

Joe was completely enchanted by the kids and performed a valuable service as coach-consultant for many of the script problems. He made his apartment available for us during the day and to me during the evening for work on the necessary transposition of songs to lower or higher keys as well as my own piano practice of the fiercely difficult score. He gave particular attention to Teddy and his opening monologue.

One of the side effects of being at Joe's was gaining time away from my phone. I had started receiving daily calls from militant teachers urging me to get out and do my duty on the picket lines. I refused and tried to explain that I did my duty to the union by not going into school, and that now my duty was to myself and my project. I was called pseudo-scab and told my project was antistrike inasmuch as it took pressure off the children's families. The late-night phone calls involving silence and heavy breathing were more amusing than frightening.

One week before the end of the strike (though we did not know it at the time) we had gone as far as we could with the show under the conditions prevailing in two small apartments. Those who had been coming regularly knew their songs, their lines, their character analysis, their makeup, and their costumes. We had accomplished everything possible without an actual stage upon which to block scenes. Further work on *Fiddler* would have been destructive as well as boring. I was not financially destroyed, but that's what I told the cast—that I could no longer afford to remain unemployed but had to find work in order to remain solvent until the strike was over. Some parents called and offered their larger Brownsville apartments to us, but no one was going to get me out into that community while the racial hates were being acted out in violence. Much later I learned of the picket-line confrontations between militant white strikers and working black teachers. The children knew we were saturated with *Fiddler* and welcomed the promised vacation.

Thus, shortly before the end of the strike, I went to work

as a temporary typist, spending eight hours a day on architectural specifications which were as dull as *Fiddler* rehearsals were exciting.

In assessing the value of these home rehearsals it was difficult to separate the way they helped the ultimate production from the way they aided the cast as individuals. Technically we could have done as well without my apartment, but the feelings that grew between me and the cast and—more important—among the members of the cast provided the magic ten percent which is the difference between excellence and perfection. Experiences were shared that were exclusive to a select group; and this gave us—there's no better word for it—a sense of family that was very real and very special.

It was natural too that we shared secrets such as the boy whose two brothers (former students of mine) were drug addicts laid up with hepatitis and forbidden entrance into city hospitals. And the girl who was frantic because her mother was living with two men in two parts of the city, playing one against the other, with the girl in between as liaison. She said, "I come from a whore and why should I even consider being anything better? I'm being what I'm from so don't try and stop me." And the boy whose mother drank up the welfare money each week, most of it going down the sink drain as her children found the bottles and broke them when she passed out. And the boy who was chained to a bed each night so that his "aunt" could ply her trade in the local bars. And the boy whose uncle provided him with women's clothing so that he could take him to a transvestite bar as his "date." And the girl who had been abandoned by her mother, leaving the daughter to be shunted from "aunt" to "aunt" and forced to steal clothing from the school's lost-and-found box. The list of the pregnant graduates grew with each confidence shared.

Many of the children were completely closed and remained

so. They had no desire to share their "other life" with us. For them it was a thrill to be accepted for exactly what they were and not be judged by conditions beyond their pale. We learned about them frame by frame starting with the realities of the present. It was their only form of freedom and I respected it.

All of us knew some of each other's background but none of us knew all of it. It was brought in, sometimes discussed, and then forgotten in the light of the theater work at hand. However, it did form a chain which might have been the essence of what gave us the fortitude to continue this innocent project through a fantastic set of circumstances which both ennobled and shamed everyone who was involved.

5

The strike continued for another few days during which I kept up daily cast contact on a personal level with the leading players, especially Teddy Smith. Despite my expectations, based on experience, planning, and faith, this potentially brilliant fourteen-year-old was not continuing to develop into the Tevye I had anticipated. He was trying, most of the time. He was prompt. He learned lines readily and took direction cautiously but well. Something or someone was getting to this boy with a force stronger than the show and more immediate than myself. Teddy was clever and consistently wrapped a protective blanket of fun-loving companionship around his personal contacts in order to discourage inquiries into his real feelings. He would drop his cheerful façade only when he believed no one was watching him.

For two years I had accepted him as a bright, articulate teen-ager whose delightful immaturity would be transformed onstage into theatrical magnetism. Teddy's audience was the world and he performed incessantly. Life was a lark—but only as long as it flew on his orders. In conflict his character changed instantly. Bursting into tears of rage he attacked, and frequently he had to be physically restrained. No distinctions were made. Girls, boys, teachers and supervisors had all been subject to his violent temper. Teddy Smith—officially Booker T. Smith—was not about to have his will defied. Until *Fiddler* I was still paying court to his illusions of adjustment. His talent more than compensated for a volatile temper.

As the excitement of first rehearsals turned into work, it became apparent that Teddy was not a dependable performer. He began to ignore appointments. He spoiled rehearsals by refusing to concentrate on character. Frequently he insisted on monotone line readings which upset his co-workers. He forgot his script and made noises to distract Beverly, his co-star.

The situation worsened and I tried to enlist the aid of other cast members to get Teddy to conform to minimum rules. It was then I realized the company did not like Teddy Smith. They were tolerating his behavior out of respect for my obvious approval of his talents. They were furious with me for backing away from confrontations. I was concerned. Too many of the show's responsibilities rested on his shoulders as the leading player. With added problems of human relations he might break. Twice our leading lady, Beverly Cannon, began to discuss Teddy's amorous advances but thought better of it. I respected her privacy. Eventually she chose the path of kindness and in her own warm way responded to his attentions as one would to an over-affectionate puppy who was to be loved and suffered. Teddy was content to label this response as "love" and delighted in the fact that gorgeous Beverly Cannon was "going" with him.

As part of the summer school's program I had taken a group of the cast to a Broadway matinee of *Fiddler on the Roof*. Since there had been nothing but praise for the standing room section at the previous week's performance of Pearl Bailey's *Hello, Dolly!*, I chose the same location for *Fiddler*.

The students were allowed to go their own way during the first act because I refused to play stage-mother. After intermission I noticed most of the boys had not returned to the theater and the second act overture was on. In fury I sped to the lavatories. There they were. Sitting and smoking. I lost my temper, not because they were smoking (about which *I* could hardly criticize them) but rather because they were missing a vital part of the show.

"How dare you," I raged. "After what I went through to get the money for this trip. And you, Teddy, with the work you have to do to even begin to break into Tevye's skin, you have the nerve to say, 'Fuck you, Mr. Piro,' and sit down here and smoke? Get upstairs! Get upstairs fast or else this is the last look you'll get of the inside of a theater for as long as you remain in my class."

Sullen and angry, they put out their cigarettes and with a familiar maddening slowness started up the stairs, all the while griping about tired feet, aching backs, and boring theater. The boys commiserated and moved into their standee positions. Teddy compromised. Instead of standing at the railing, he chose to sit on the stairs leading up to the balcony. I knew and he knew that I knew that he could therefore see only a fraction of the stage action, including the Tevye monologue that was then going on. His rebellion, as usual, was calculated to enrage me but I avoided a confrontation. He was apt to walk out of the theater. We were on an official school trip and I would have to catch him and bring him back. He might have made a loud scene there in the orchestra section. I looked around at the fidgeting boys and girls. They faced the stage but were neither seeing nor hearing. I really couldn't blame them. They were shrewd enough in theater *savoir-faire* to sense a performance unworthy of their attention and were totally unschooled in hiding boredom. I thought in panic, "If a less than perfect professional *Fiddler on the Roof* is boring to a cast intimately familiar with its problems, won't it be stupid to ask our Brooklyn audiences to respond positively to a single viewing? My God, it won't work."

Just before leaving I promised each of the children that our production would be infinitely better than the one we had just seen.

A few days later Bruce Birnel bought box seats for his student lighting crew. He denied that this venture was a personal extravagance, insisting that it was necessary for these boys to get as close to the technical aspects of the show as possible. I asked Bruce to include Teddy as well as Maritza, our Hodel, who had missed the previous trip. After the show, the group came to my apartment for an après-theater Coke. Their comments were scathing.

"Boy, was it lousy," shouted Brucie Ampolsky, our student technical chief.

"Mr. Piro, nobody even bothered to talk to anyone on stage. They were all in a vacuum," David Hamilton said.

Another youngster declared, "The musical numbers were so fast you couldn't even understand the words."

"Teddy, what did you learn from their Tevye?" I asked.

"I learned exactly what not to do."

By this time most of the group had removed their coats. I looked at Maritza Figueroa. Dark brown hair fell softly to her shoulders, framing a pale complexion, and making her large eyes even brighter. I realized that I knew nothing about this young lady outside of experiences in my classroom. She and the other Puerto Rican girls had not attended the home rehearsals. Maritza, like Teddy, was tolerated—he for his compulsive humor and she for being pushy.

Maritza entered through the group. While they paused in the doorway, she moved to the most prominent chair in the room and sat on the edge, huddled up inside her matching spring coat. Her eyes were downcast.

"Hey, Marooch," I called. "You goin' to stay a while?"

"That's OK, Mr. Piro," she said in a thick Spanish accent, "I keep my coat on and help you."

She then padded into the kitchen and took over the cake-slicing and started the hot chocolate. Bruce looked at me.

"What's going on with her?"

"I don't know, Bruce. She's obviously doing a sketch and doing it very well. I love it."

For the remainder of the evening she continued playing the role of a maiden aunt who gets all the work and suffers in silence. We ignored her acting, which brought her to further exaggeration of each suffering gesture.

The group assembled for the ride home. I heard Teddy making farewells.

"Teddy," I asked, "aren't you driving back to Brooklyn with Mr. Birnel?"

"No. I'm taking the A train up to my grandmother's in Harlem."

"Oh, no, you're not! It's after midnight. I can't afford to lose you to a drug addict between Brownsville and Harlem. We don't need Teddy Smith, but the show does. When we close you can go wherever you like whenever the spirit moves you. But now de spirit says that you're staying with the group."

We tried keeping the tone light, but a confrontation was brewing. The group adjusted their now-they're-at-it-again faces of tolerance. As an out, I suggested we call his mother to verify permission. I had to be covered. He agreed and dialed home. I started for the phone. He moved his head in a subtle gesture to stop me.

"I'll talk to her," I insisted, and took the receiver forcefully from his hand. He knew my pressure points and the uselessness of argument. As I moved into the kitchen with the phone he pulled the group to the other side of the living room, out of earshot. Finally, after several rings, Mrs. Smith answered. I explained the situation and waited for her to respond. She didn't. Since it was late Saturday night I thought no more about it and hung up.

"Teddy, your mother doesn't know anything about your going to your grandmother's, so Mr. Birnel will drive you home with the others."

He started to object but then checked himself, grabbed the phone, and dialed. We were momentarily stunned with the swiftness of his actions. Then, moving into the center of the group, he began a bright running conversation by relating the evening's adventures, the quality of the show, the refreshments, and a fast rationale for his going up to Harlem on the subway. At times he listened and nodded his head. He hung up with a cheery "See you in the morning." There was nothing I could do at the moment. I made an appointment to see him the next afternoon and bid them all good-night.

The next day Teddy arrived two hours late. He related how he had gone home first and got "tied up."

"Why the hell did you go all the way from Harlem to Brooklyn and back to Manhattan when you could have stopped off right here in the middle?" I asked.

"I told you. Because I had to see my mother and brothers."

"Couldn't you have called them?"

"I did and there wasn't any answer. Look, Mr. Piro, didn't I come here to learn how to do makeup?"

"Oh, Teddy. I thought you came to be with me on a lonely Sunday afternoon."

"Sheee-it. Can we start, please?"

He was upset and apparently did not care to offer a cover story for his acts. Whatever situation he had encountered that morning had cut deeper than most. His timing was off. My instinct urged, "Now that he's this strung out I can get behind the mask. We're alone with no threat of interruptions."

I continued exploring his need for going home first. Running out of flippant remarks he finally blurted out, "Because when I called home this morning there wasn't any answer!"

"You said that before, Teddy. Maybe she went for a walk, or to church. It's a lovely day, or didn't you notice in your flight?"

"What fright? I didn't say anything about being scared."

"Then you were scared? Scared of what?"

"Who said. . . ?"

"You did. I said 'flight' and you picked up 'fright' and added 'scared.' That's where it's at, isn't it?"

"Look, if you said . . ."

"What scared you, Teddy? Come on. It's OK."

"I . . ."

"What scared you, Teddy?"

"My little brothers, Scooter and Derek."

"Your little brothers?"

"No. I was scared *for* them. My mother couldn't have gone out. She can never get up that early. Look. Either we do make-up or I go home!"

It was a start. There was time. I began laying out makeup, then built his beard while explaining the process. I showed him how to straighten out crepe hair and then apply wisps of it to his face with liquid latex. The trick was to vary the shades of white to black so that it appeared like a graying process. The next step was for him to apply the makeup by himself enough times so that results were planned and not accidental.

While he was engrossed in this task I again started questioning. He spilled a glass of soda on his trousers, which necessitated his leaving the room and changing into my robe. He placed the damp trousers on a sofa over towels to dry. I watched him. Progress had been made. For the first time in our association he had physically retreated from confrontation. Again I gave in, but was determined to see this situation through before he left my home.

He finished making up. I suggested we sit and talk while he got accustomed to the annoying pull of a false beard. There was nothing he could do. He was sitting comfortably in the reclining chair with a fresh soda by his side. He had just checked his drying trousers for creases. I was seated opposite him.

"Teddy," I began. His head was turned away looking out the window, trying to seem casual but bristling with alertness. The light heightened his Afro-style hair. His full lips were pursed in caution, accentuating the flare of his nostrils.

"Teddy, would you look at me?" I said. He slowly turned his head. The light turned his warm brown skin into a copper glow.

"Last night I spoke with your mother, but she didn't respond."

He was ready for this one.

"Oh, she told me to tell you she was sorry about that. You got her out of bed. When I called back she was wide awake. You heard us talking?"

"I heard you talking, Teddy. It was an Academy Award performance, star."

He started to get off the chair.

"Gotta check my pants."

I put my hand out to stop him.

"Mr. Piro!"

"Whether you like it or not we are going to talk."

"Mr. Piro, I don't want to."

"You are not responsible for your mother," I yelled.

For the first time he looked directly into my eyes, briefly, then turned back toward the window.

"Teddy, look at me." He refused.

"I'll say it again more slowly. You are fourteen years old. You live with an older sister and two little brothers, Derek and Scooter. You are devoted to your brothers, no?"

"Yes."

"And it's beautiful watching you with them—the love that flows from you. It's much too beautiful a thing to bother playing games. I'm not playing. I won't. Teddy, you are not responsible for your mother."

"I still don't know what you mean."

"Teddy, the panic you just put into that line indicates you know goddamned well what I mean, so let's cut out all of this shit and for once get down to where it's at. I promise you, I sincerely promise you, that I will never bring this subject up again if we get to the bottom of it now. OK, you are not responsible for your mother. Why are you protecting her?"

He put his head down and took in a great breath of air. I waited. The silence grew.

Softly I said, "Teddy, it's OK to cry. Real men cry. Want to talk about it?"

"No," he shouted. "I don't want to talk about it! I'm sick of it. Do you really want to know why I didn't come on time today? Because when I called home I couldn't get no answer and I got scared for Derek and Scooter. I *had* to go home to see if . . . I'm not responsible for my mother? OK, then tell me who's responsible for my brothers? Remember when you called up the other day and Derek said my mother couldn't come to the phone? Well, he was right. So when I'm not there to make their breakfasts they don't eat. When I'm not there to do the laundry they don't have clean clothes. And when you call a rehearsal and I can't go shopping, they don't get much dinner." Uncontrolled tears were rolling down his face. "Do you know why I'm absent so often from school? Because she goes out and don't tell me when she's coming back so I have to take care of the kids, that's why."

"What about your older sister? Why doesn't Kim take some of these responsibilities?"

"Because she don't care. She says, 'I have to go to school so I'm going.' So who does that leave? Sometimes when my mother goes out I can't call you to tell you because she puts a lock on the phone and takes the key with her."

I gripped his shoulders.

"Teddy. She's using you. You're a victim, can't you see? She's clever, your mother, and realizes that she has a son who is a warm, responsible, sensitive human being and she's squeezing your balls with it. She's using your wonderfulness to destroy you. It's not a new story. She knows full well that Kim won't buy any of this victimization shit because Kim is going to go about her business of growing up. But with you—she's got you. And unless you do something about it you're going to remain a little boy doing a man's job for the rest of your life. And still you defend her. Why?"

"Because she's my mother!"

"Bullshit. She's an adult human being and you're fourteen. What makes you feel you have to take care of her?"

"I *don't* take care of her. I take care of my little brothers."

"What would happen if you simply said, 'Mother, I have responsibilities to myself and I will not play guardian to my little brothers. That's your job. I'm going to go to school every day and live my own life from now on.' "

"I don't know."

"Are you willing to try it?"

"No."

"That brings us back to where we started, doesn't it?"

"I guess so."

"Teddy, how would you like to leave your house and go somewhere else to live? It's possible, you know. One phone call to the right people and your mother's game will be over."

He shook his head, trying to brush away the tears, not even thinking about this new possibility. It was *his* mother and *his* little brothers. Good or bad, this private hell had to be endured.

I moved to get tissues and he rose from the chair to check

his dry trousers, refusing my offer. We both paused, wary. I had done my best. It was out in the open and the next move would have to come from him. Immature? School provided his only chance of being a little boy—at home survival demanded manhood. I made the decision to speak to Mrs. Seitzer in the morning and ask for official and personal counseling opinions of the situation and to demand no action unless conditions became intolerable for Teddy. Right now we could live with it as long as he was able to maintain a double life as father to a family and happy-go-lucky teen-ager in a show production.

He pulled himself together and removed his makeup. I suggested he do it once more. He did, and I was amazed at his creativity in making himself, a black child, into a middle-aged Russian Jew. He joked about possible neighborhood encounters if he chose to go home in makeup. The subject of mother and brothers became taboo. We never spoke of them again, as I had promised. Something warned me that the situation may not have been as bleak as he painted. Perhaps he was making the most of two enviable positions, coming to school only when he felt like it and having what he considered an airtight excuse for his own considerable laziness. All the teachers were familiar with his ability to create stunning lies when threatened with a loss of image.

"Teddy, do you trust me?" I asked softly.

"I . . . No."

"Is there anyone you can be straight with?"

"No."

"Do you ever want or wish that there was someone that you could talk to? I mean, really talk to?"

"No. I can do it myself."

"Come on. I'll help you take the makeup off. It's unprofessional to walk the streets with it on."

I thought, here is a young boy ripe for drugs, or a brilliant career in the theater. Perhaps both. The pattern was not new.

6

A week later, shortly before Thanksgiving, a vote was called to ratify an agreement which ended the longest strike in educational history.

The staff that returned to Junior High School 275 was typical: It contained a few sadists who despised the children and used the classroom or gym as a private kingdom in which to indulge their frustrations; a few supremely effective individuals to whom teaching was a totally involving life of service; a few middle-class blacks who could not accept the ghetto child because of cultural disparities in background. There were some successful black teachers who performed on the concept of service to their own people—they had beaten the system and broken out of the mold; their job was to insure others would follow. There was a group of sharp young men for whom education was the diversion which allowed them ample time to pursue other financially rewarding ventures. They did their jobs with little imagination and lots of attention to union contracts which dictated class sizes, extra pay for extra duties, the number of periods to be assigned in the week, and seniority and, in general, prided themselves on their "professionalism." They were strong union supporters pledged to lift the status of the profession from patient, underpaid service, to equality with those earning European vacations in the business world. We had a few husband-seekers and several married ladies who were divided between their own family concerns and the need to do meaningful work outside of their homes. These women were effective, sympathetic teachers. The staff of Junior High School 275 had two things in common: Most of them were Jews and most had been born, educated, and trained as teachers in New York City. Few, if any, were totally free of inherited prejudices, including one which said that black children couldn't learn.

A New York City public school is similiar to a New York City apartment building where "neighbor" is a fact of physical placement only. I have no compulsion to fraternize with the residents on my floor; a nod on the elevator is enough. The teacher in an adjoining classroom receives the same nod. I have my music room, my children, and my particular curriculum problems; and unless a colleague is directly involved through supervision or guidance, we may share the same lunch table without conversation. To a few on the staff I am a friend. To several I am a distinguished colleague, but to most I'm a stranger. Socially I was intimate with Guidance Counselor Irene Seitzer and Health Education Teacher Olivia Stukes, but saw a few others on weekends only when school business required a shared project. This was unfortunate and totally different from the average school in America, where the term "faculty" implies working together as a team for the same purpose.

A chief concern on that first poststrike morning was to protect my mobility in moving from group to group. Would I enjoy the freedom to remain a loner, picking social contacts on an individual basis rather than as a member of a faction? Or would I be imprisoned by a category? Militant unionists had made insulting phone calls to get me on the picket lines.

They also had hurled invective at the nonstriking black teachers. Both strikers and workers held in contempt those of us who had met with children outside of school. We were cowards who had compromised in a time of deadly choice.

I walked into the faculty room for morning coffee. The room lacked its usual healthy din. The polarization of groups was chilling, each faction pretending the other did not exist. Between the black and union tables sat the smallest group, mine, looking amused and innocent since they had cleverly avoided both labels—"scab" and "child-killer." I greeted my own faction, got coffee, and sat with the blacks, who were nearer to the urn.

"Hi, Olivia," I said.

"Good morning, Dick," she responded, formally.

The chatter fluttered to a standstill. Someone was jumping his category. Curiosity was apparent. Imitating Olivia's liquid voice, I sat down and mimicked, "Good morning, Dick. Miss Gym Teacher worked and made so much money that she's gone high-class to the starving music-drama teacher."

The black teachers laughed. It was a healthy sign which reduced some tension. Olivia Stukes was a stunning young woman in her middle twenties. Her fashionably thin figure was further streamlined by simple clothes, no makeup, and comfortably short Afro-style hair. Her one excess was large walnut-framed glasses which sat on her face at nostril level, almost blending with her rich, dark coloring. A graduate of Fisk University, Olivia was impatient to have all she was entitled to in life, including a successful second career as a dancer, model, singer, and actress. She anticipated fabulous wealth and in preparation had recently moved away from her parents and now lived in a tiny six-flight walk-up apartment in West Greenwich Village. Her preparation went slowly but steadily. Proper pronunciation of French vegetables became as important as voice coaching. Olivia's sense of humor was accompanied by an even greater sense of honesty. As part of a master plan in theater arts, she had volunteered to assist in the production of *Fiddler on the Roof,* and studiously watched the Jewish Hour on Sunday-morning television. Her specific function was choreography.

"Livia," I went on, "are we going to pretend we didn't speak on the phone every night since this bloody strike began or will we groove on the fact that we have choreography to do for this Friday's assemblies?"

"Friday?" she gasped.

"That's right, jockstrap, in four days."

"But—"

"I know. Only four days. But I think we can do 'Tradition.' It just means work."

"Gee, I don't know."

"I suspect some people have been working to stop *Fiddler.* If we can hit them with this number and demonstrate exactly what we're up to then maybe some of these ridiculous fears of Jewish accents and gestures will be seen for what they are—stupid."

"Isn't that something." This was Olivia's catchall phrase which meant she needed a moment to think. The conversation was being observed and evaluated by the other teachers in the room. We were stepping over a line that some had vowed would not be crossed.

"I'm sorry, Dick, but I can't be there after school today."

The tension in the room abated.

"But," she went on quickly, "I'll be there all the other days. I've arranged my schedule so that I can help you during all the in-school rehearsal periods. I have lunch then anyway."

The smiles froze and eyebrows arched.

She continued, "Gee, I'm sorry. I made other plans for today. I didn't think you'd be ready so soon."

"That's OK. How are you going home?" I asked.

"With Shelly. I haven't talked to him since the strike

began, but I'm sure he's still driving downtown every day."

"Damn," I said. "Maybe I'll give the kids the afternoon off and go with you. I miss our joy ride. Besides I need some more beard makings and there's a drug store right near you that sells theatrical makeup."

"Can't I get it for you?"

"No, thanks. I want very specific stuff. I don't know the names for the colors so I'll have to see it myself. Are you leaving right after dismissal?"

"Yeah. Listen, if I don't see you at lunch, meet Shelly and me by the side door. I'll be in a hurry so don't get hung up with the kids."

A few minutes after three-o'clock dismissal, Olivia walked up to me, hooked her arm in mine, and gently pulled me towards the main entrance.

"Where you going?" I resisted. "Shelly parks on the other side of the building."

"Come on. I'll tell you on the way to the train."

"The train? But you said we were driving."

"Let's go."

"I am not going to walk five blocks until I know why I can't ride in an air-conditioned car. Tell me."

"I can't."

"Olivia Stukes!"

"OK," she said.

I unlocked the empty auditorium and we stepped into its welcome coolness. I searched her face. She wasn't so much angry as shocked and amused. With a delicately manicured index finger she pushed her glasses higher on her nose and announced, "Shelly just told me that he wasn't supposed to take any scabs home in his car."

Shelly was a young white teacher then doing an excellent job. He was bright, articulate, and deeply involved with one of the school's most defeated classes.

"Livia," I scoffed, "that's stupid. Shelly is very much his

own man. You must have heard wrong. He certainly has the intelligence to separate his political feelings from social contacts."

I could see that she was hurt. I started towards the doors.

"Liv," I ordered, "go out the other door and I'll meet you in five minutes outside. I'm going to find Shelly."

She did as I asked. I waited a second and then headed towards the general office. Shelly was talking to some teachers standing near the time clock. As I approached he said, "Hi, Dick. Coming to the city?"

"Yeah. But where's Olivia? She wanted to come with us."

"Ah, she won't be coming along any more."

"How come?" I asked, innocently.

"Well . . ." he fumbled. "She just won't be joining us, that's all there is to it."

"Shelly, I can't believe it. Then it's true what she just told me?"

"I don't know what she's told you but she won't be with us from now on, period."

"Shelly, I—"

"Look, are you coming or not? I'm in a hurry."

He picked up his attaché case and started to turn away.

"Shelly?" I called.

"What?" he turned.

"Tell your union gorillas to go fuck themselves!"

I turned heel and left the office to meet Olivia outside. I was furious. This man did not measure up to the standards I had thought he would. How could such a good teacher allow himself to be manipulated? I started feeling contempt. Olivia did her thing during the strike by working every day. I did mine by rehearsing with kids at home. Shelly did his by carrying a picket sign. Hostilities were over for Liv and me, but why did they have to go on for Shelly? We all had enjoyed the trip driving into the Village, frequently stopping for a drink. I met Olivia and silently we walked to the subway. It was our last social encounter with Shelly Katz.

Since Dr. Robbins had not been informed of our midstrike change from *The Crucible* to *Fiddler on the Roof,* I kept myself near his office during the next two days, hoping for an invitation to discuss my plans. I needed his official sanction, confirmation of performance dates, and, especially, approval for the almost-certain ABC documentary film. I did not invoke my right as a department head to demand a meeting, preferring an approach from him. He was courteous when we passed each other in the halls. But he made no reference to our theater plans. I tried to understand his silence about the drama program.

"When he wants to see us, Bruce, he will," I said. "Since we haven't heard anything negative, let's just go on with the show and assume his support. I think he expects us to. When his science, math, and history problems are solved he'll get to us. We should be flattered that he hasn't given us the usual pep talk about 'business as usual.' "

It was an exciting week for *Fiddler on the Roof*. After rehearsals in the confinement of Joe's apartment and mine, the cast bloomed and frolicked on the vastness of the school's stage. The Puerto Rican girls who for unknown reasons had not attended home rehearsals joined us and progressed rapidly, soon catching up with the others. One of the duties of the assistant principal, Amelia Brown, was filling an assembly schedule. She was overjoyed with my offer to perform on Friday. Although it was mid-November, for all practical purposes we were once again in the first week of school. Our assembly performance was important. The plan was to present the opening production number—"Tradition"—with costumes, some basic lighting, and a suggestion of makeup. It was an obvious ploy to gain teacher support by exposing all central characters within the framework of what many consider the best piece of writing in the show. Teachers who feared ridicule of Jews would have an opportunity to investigate my intended directing style. The ethnic beauty of Joe Stein's script lay not in accents but rather in traditional speech rhythms. Here rested the "Jewishness." I thought it would be most clear to Jews themselves. I sympathized with their sensitivity and looked forward to calming the fears.

This assembly was vital for Teddy Smith. His latest rebellion was to refuse to pull out all the stops with Tevye. He felt it was a waste of talent to "perform" in rehearsal. I had little faith or trust in his actor's discipline. We were working with a taped orchestral background and he could easily destroy the number. Given an approving audience, his tendency was to mug and show off. He was a delightful showman but as a character in a serious, albeit humorous, drama, his routine was demoralizing to the rest of the cast and offensive to me. His Tevye was still very much that of a super-talented fourteen-year-old comic *playing* the role. As one of the most difficult characterizations in modern musical theater, Tevye must be a comic who sees everything through the eyes of a performer. Teddy was unable and unwilling to go from Teddy to Tevye and leave it there. He insisted in going from Teddy to Tevye and then back to Teddy. His worst performance would satisfy any audience, but I was pledged to a show and not to a star.

Tuesday, Wednesday, and Thursday were frantic days of pressure. I had been totally honest with the children and they accepted the fact that the future of their show rested upon Friday's assemblies. They worked hard and diligently. A call was placed for black frock coats and yarmulkes—the skullcaps worn by orthodox Jews. On Tuesday evening we had our first *Fiddler* miracle. I went to the incinerator room of my apartment building to empty trash. There, neatly piled on the floor, were five black coats a neighbor was discarding. With a little sewing they suited our needs perfectly. I put a note on the wall asking for more, and the following morning five additional coats were placed outside my door. Brucie Ampolsky and Steven Hirsch, our only two real Jews in the production, provided the black and white yarmulkes.

Early Friday morning found an excited crew already assembled for costumes and makeup. They were anxious to perform for the eighth-graders—their peers. It was an honor to have been selected for drama, and this was their first opportunity to show off. I entered the building shortly after 7:30 A.M. and the children greeted me raucously with "Mazeltov" and "Shalom." I handed my container of coffee to Duane and opened the door to the prop room. This was our special place. Technically it was a storage area for costumes, properties, and scenery, but we made it the nerve center of theater activity. The makeup was placed in the middle of the L-shaped room. Boys and girls changed into costumes separately at the two ends of the room, but there was much bumping traffic as they gathered at the middle to observe and be observed. Having been involved with previous productions, most of the children had long lost typical teen-age reactions to the opposite sex in various states of undress. New children quickly caught on that we didn't play the usual games.

"An actor's body is no more sexual to the actor than the wrench is to the plumber," I preached. "Your body is a tool you need for work. If you can't accept this when preparing for a performance, you don't belong here. Boys, if you want to peep at titty then head for Coney Island. Girls, I want to know when and if you are bothered."

Initially the cast retired to the far ends of the room to undress. By the third session they used the center of the room so as to be closer to makeup and to be able to apply it while putting on wigs, costumes, and hats. Inhibitions decreased and the prop room was transformed into a professional-appearing dressing room complete with boys dressed only in undershorts and girls in slips and bras. No nonsense. Only business. While it was never expressed, I felt many children, boys especially, were relieved not to have to play sex games—which were already a bore since most, by this time, had experienced full sexual initiation.

Contrary to my directions, the children assisted each other in making up. Because of his special beard requirements, Teddy had his own equipment, which he set up in a star corner.

For this performance I paid particular attention to the dressing of the Rabbi. Paul (Rabbi) Marzen was a big enough person to accept constant teasing. We referred to him as "our very own Puerto Rican troll." He was less than four feet tall and chattered constantly with a Spanish accent. A slight speech impediment gave him difficulty starting certain words; he covered it up by stuttering a rapid "Ah." His makeup was simple: a white Santa Claus wig falling down to his shoulders; a beard reaching to his navel; a black frock coat reaching to his ankles; and a pair of rubber boots which, he complained, reached to his arm pits. Topping the outfit was a black fedora hat. He carried an enormous book (*The Oxford Dictionary*) disguised as a Bible. As the Rabbi Paul had few lines, but as a delightful character he could steal the show. In the Broadway company, many complained that the Rabbi was played as a buffoon. Dr. Robbins prevented my script deletions by convincing me that poking fun at the rabbi was a favorite sport of Yiddish writers.

Paul was serious with his makeup. As each item was attached his chatter decreased. He gently placed the hat over the scratchy wig, took a final look into the mirror, and was quiet. I watched as he found an uncluttered spot in the prop room. From there he sat and watched the group, benevolent and with infinite wisdom. "My God," I thought, "he's become a rabbi before the first performance." I looked at the other boys. Gradually, as they completed their individual preparations, they too assumed poses and altered their speech patterns, becoming Jews. I waited for the jokes. There were none. I became "Reb Piro" for all.

The signal was given for stage places. There was no nervousness. We were solid on this much of the show. These performers were much too unsophisticated to feign stage fright when they felt none. The house lights dimmed and from the tape recorder in the pit I started the *Fiddler* theme. The curtain rose to show a blank stage. On floor level right a door opened and a single spot picked up Teddy, wearily climbing the four steps to the stage. He had on a dairyman's cap, knickers, high boots, vest, and a grey shirt. He paused, chewed on a corner of his beard, looked at the audience and took off the granny glasses as if to clean them. He said, "A fiddler on the roof? Sounds crazy, no? Well, in our little village of Anatevka, you might say that every one of us is a fiddler on the roof trying to scratch out a simple living. It isn't easy!"

"Contact," I whispered. In panic I realized he wasn't playing to the audience, but to the vacuum between his nose and the first row. This was his specialty, to see nothing as he imagined an adoring audience of thousands. He responded to my SOS by glaring at the audience. We heard a snicker. Teddy played the rest of the monologue to that spot of darkness where he had heard the giggle. After explaining the customs in the village of Anatevka he led into the song, "Tradition." Here the delicate fiddler theme leaped into a stirring peasant rhythm as the ensemble appeared on both sides of the stage, hands joined and held high. They danced in single files, singing the word "Tradition." The lines crossed, snaked around, and eventually formed a large circle which Teddy joined.

The cast were completely turned on by this music and, in keeping with their own dance styles, had previously insisted on going into a deep knee-bending, shoulder-shaking Afro routine that was hilarious but totally wrong for the show. I had allowed them to play with it as a loosening-up device, forgetting that most basic of teacher maxims: "It is almost impossible to unlearn." I then tried unsuccessfully to bring the choreography from Afro to Jewish, wanting it simple and dignified but also joyous. We fought. The day before, I had kept the ensemble long beyond promised dismissal time. We did the dance again and again and again. My hope was to exhaust them to a point where they would forget the Afro embellishments and simply do it straight, at which point I could scream, "That's it! Do it that way all the time." But they did not become tired. Instead they got angry and with chins held high they danced off the stage in fury. That rehearsal was successful. Watching this opening performance I saw them push all Afro movements inside; but in spite of the surface indications of perfect Russian Jews, their attitudes bubbled out revealing a pride and joy, an absolute security in their identities. This was a brilliant moment where the mixture of music, movement, and text combined with an ethnic reality to produce simply people. This was *theater*.

After a few moments my instincts indicated that this performance would ring the bell. As I watched, my mind kept returning to the events of the previous two days. On Wednesday, I had walked into a volcanic faculty room for morning coffee. On the subway I had read *The New York Times* coverage of the controversy raging over a tasteless anti-Semitic poem that had been read by a black man on the listener-sponsored FM radio station WBAI. The poem began, "Hey there, Jew boy, with your yarmulke on your head." The city was up in arms and Federal Communications Commission authorities had been approached by several angry Jews to revoke WBAI's license. The station defended its right to air all sides of every issue.

At Junior High School 275 teachers glared at me. Someone threw a copy of the *Times* on my table growling, "See? Do you still have any doubt where we stand with niggers?"

Those who had previously refused to become involved in the *Fiddler* controversy now announced their disapproval. The remaining fence-sitters had disappeared. Few fell over to my side. Not wishing to cope with the hostility, I left the room to type a memo for Dr. Robbins.

"I realize you have been too busy to see me," I wrote, "but please, please do not make any decisions concerning *Fiddler on the Roof* until you see our presentation at the Friday eighth-grade assemblies."

Two periods later the memo was returned with an ominous note scribbled in black marking pen across the top: "See me Period 6." Since Periods 4 and 5 were unassigned on my schedule (both lunch periods) I went into the faculty room to wait. Something was up, but I felt ready. I settled into a conversation with Bernice Rosen, an English teacher who, while strongly opposed to the project, was still a good friend. Our communication flowed freely. The door burst open and Mitchell Grossman stormed in, backed by three male colleagues whose names I did not know. He slammed *The New York Times* down in front of me.

"Are you still going through with it?" he asked trying patiently to suppress his anger.

"Naturally, Mitch. I abhor what this is all about, but I'm absolutely certain we're doing something positive to change it. The poem, I mean."

"I'm asking you again and you'd better think about it. Are you going on with *Fiddler on the Roof*?"

"Mitch, now what can I say? You know my answer has to be yes. Being dramatic is my thing, not yours."

"We're going to fight you, Piro, and we're going to win. Last year you proved your anti-Semitism with *Oliver!* Fagin is one thing but an entire cast of Fagins staggers the imagination. You're not getting away with this one. We're going to get you and destroy you. Your work days in this school are over—and in any other school after we're through."

"Mitch, I appreciate this," I said as softly as possible, embarrassed by his emotionalism. "Thanks for the warning. I'm glad you're heading the opposition and not that creep who tried to stop *Oliver!* I can talk to you reasonably. We'll fight and one of us will win and, you know, I'll enjoy every minute of it. It's this very kind of thing that makes my work exciting. Thanks for the interest, if not the agony."

I resumed eating, hoping he would leave. He stood as if stunned. Finally, he asked, "Tell me one thing, Mr. Piro. Would you have presented *Fiddler on the Roof* in Yorkville during the height of the Nazi Party convention?"

Since I had no idea where Yorkville was or any knowledge of a Nazi Party convention (weren't they still illegal?) I remained silent, looking for an answer that would not broadcast my ignorance. Before I could reply, Mitch turned and started out of the room saying, "He doesn't have an answer for that one, does he?" The door slammed, and for a moment the room was silent. The conversational buzz resumed. Bernice looked shocked, her love for me showing conflict with what she must have considered a crude but just declaration of war from Mitch, her ally. I waited, expecting some teachers to come over and express displeasure with such tactics. No one moved. I said to Bernice, "I can't believe it. I simply do not believe what's going on. How can you and Mitch even dream of turning away from this terrible thing? It's out, damn it! The whole city is screaming about black anti-Semitism. I hate it. But, I'm going to *do* something about it, not just moan and cry and feel persecuted."

Abruptly Bernice stabbed her knife in the air and said angrily, "It's fine for Italo-American glamour boy Piro to speak of strength. We're scared. Do you understand that? Can you? They hate us. Our jobs are being taken away. Blacks and Puerto Ricans are going to the top of all supervisory-candidate lists. It's not the time to wave Jewish banners in black faces. We can't afford the charge of ramming Jewish culture down the kids' throats. Let's forget 'Jewish' and hope it goes away. Later, when things calm down, we can quietly work out anti-Semitic problems with the community in our own way, without fanfare."

"Bunny, I love you and I admire you but I simply do not understand. Why doesn't Mitch fight the source of this thing with the same vengeance he intends to fight me? Why aren't you willing to stick your necks out? Has retreat ever solved anything? The one thing Hitler taught us is that appeasement never solved a problem permanently. I thought turning the other cheek was a Christian concept. Fight *them,* damn it, not *me.* I'm on your side. Use me. I have more power than all of you."

"What power?"

"I'm not a Jew. It's that simple. And I'm going to fight this thing through even if you knock my teeth out in the process."

Whatever reply Bernice had prepared was cut short by the bell. I entered Dr. Robbins' office with the secure feeling of having a solid argument for continuing the show. I was absolutely certain he would delay a decision at least until Friday's performance, two days hence—he owed us that much. Dr. Robbins indicated a chair, opened a desk drawer and took out an ashtray. He avoided eye contact. I sensed defeat, and the ulcer I had carried for the past ten years sent out a warning signal.

"Dick," he began, "I won't keep you in suspense. I am canceling the production of *Fiddler on the Roof.*"

"But—"

"Until the highest authorities in the Brownsville Community Council assure me in writing that they are receptive to this project it must remain canceled. I will not risk racial reprisals. I know you've been in touch with Lil Carter and some other parents. But I will not be satisfied with support from them. They're plugging for you and don't speak for the entire community. Their elected officials do."

I settled back to listen. His line of reasoning had obviously been prepared. I tuned back in.

"Even you must be aware," he was saying, "that the strike has placed us in a most delicate situation. The community feels that we are out to feather our own nests and don't give a damn for the kids. All the trust and faith we once shared with the community has gone down the drain. The staff is broken into three factions, and it will be a long, long time—if ever—before we enjoy the unity that we had between black and white. Now you ask me to add still another division? I'm not going to do it. Before the strike I had my doubts but was willing to gamble on your personal support pushing the thing through, but I have no right now to take that risk. Therefore, you will continue rehearsing until after Friday's assemblies and then quietly phase out the project. You can give the difficulty of getting rights as our official excuse, and reinstate *The Crucible* as the major spring show."

I first felt sick, then angered, and finally numb, looking at this man whom I loved and respected. His face was expressionless.

"Dr. Robbins, I have no choice but to follow your directive."

"That's right."

"But I must express my deepest disappointment at the idea that I'm working for a Jew. I thought I worked for a principal."

He looked up sharply but restrained whatever he was about to say. My remark stung him, as I intended it to.

"Don't you realize that you're doing what you all claimed never to do?" I argued. "You're making *Jewish* decisions. You're justifying every racist charge the community is making against you. You're running scared. Your Jewish staff is led by teachers that, if you could, you'd remove for having consistently failed in their jobs. Now what are you doing? You're letting them fuck up your job. Forget about me. Forget the kids and the months we put into this show. Forget the ABC film that's in the works. Forget the expenses Bruce has personally gone to in buying the most sophisticated lighting equipment available. How casually you wipe it all out. If anything comes from the community it will be this: Why did we cancel something that was judged educationally valid six months ago?"

Dr. Robbins made no reply. Instead, he allowed me to go on until I had run out of steam. He then reminded me that I had been consistently winning controversies for four years.

"Look, Dick," he said. "You managed to move mountains to get your Massachusetts exchange trip going. You've won all of your battles against impossible odds. Isn't it about time you lost one? It's a simple case of statistics. Win ten, lose one. I've made my decision. You have work to do."

I left as abruptly as possible, afraid that the philosophic aspects of the argument would deteriorate into personal antagonism. Oddly enough, I was not convinced that this was the end of *Fiddler*. I would simply have to add Robbins to the opposition and go through the war without his support. I still had the project in hand—at least until Friday. I had lost only Robbins. I was furious and absolutely certain, at that point, that the militant Jews had gotten to him; and I was ashamed for having been tactically outmaneuvered. Couldn't I have gotten to him first? I headed towards the faculty room to pick up my briefcase and find a quiet corner in which to plan the next move.

As I opened the door I heard solid laughter. Mitchell Grossman was standing with a group of people. They stopped and looked up. Bernice looked pained. Reason and logic? I broke. "Since you refuse to fight," I shouted across the room to Bernice, "I can only conclude that you deserved what you got throughout history, and unless you stiffen up you are more than deserving of what you're going to get!" I stormed out.

Within minutes most of the staff were informed of my half-quote: "The Jews deserved what they got throughout history." With such bald, obvious proof of my rampant anti-Semitism, the last outposts of support deserted the project, including nearly all the Gentile staff. It was stupid to have given in to rage. Up until then I was unaware of the degree to which my feelings were tied to *Fiddler on the Roof*.

Later that day Amelia Brown sought me out as part of her school-community-relations responsibilities and attempted to mend fences. Reason had returned and I endured her kindness, but was anxious to be alone or with cast members, not with an assistant principal.

"Look, Dick," she cautioned. "You can't fly off the handle like that and expect to accomplish anything. Now I support you and all of your ideas. I especially support *Fiddler,* you know that. Didn't I take *Oliver!* to my Human Relations course and iron out all of your difficulties? In order to best help you now, I cannot support this project openly. That will place me on a side. I'm going to remain publicly neutral and privately help you plan things out. We'll go through with it as you wish. But please try to remember this. You are not dealing with intelligent, rational people right now. You have a cause and it's anti-Semitism. For us Jews, it is something very real. Since we're scared, we are going to react illogically, irrationally, and—most important—emotionally. Now, tell me exactly what happened in the office with the boss."

I related Robbins' conversation, and towards the end Amelia was grinning. I didn't like it.

"Dick Piro," she laughed, "you've worked for the boss for four years. I can't believe that you've finally been fooled by him."

My head began to spin and I gripped the arms of the chair to counteract the sensation of floating.

"Now tell me," she said. "What was he really saying?"

"Amelia!" I burst out. "It's incredible. He said he couldn't help me because he was caught between his staff and the community. But I knew what to do and how to do it. I had proved this before. He told me to go out and fight. And win!"

"Exactly!" she said, very pleased.

I wanted to hug her. I wanted to hug Dr. Robbins and I wanted to hug Mitchell Grossman. My team was intact and *Fiddler* would go on as planned.

I was high when I started off to meet my next class. Mitch was approaching from the other end of the corridor. Filled with magnanimity I approached him saying, "You know, Mitch, we almost have a comic-operetta situation here. I'm of Sicilian Roman Catholic heritage. I've worked with Jews most of my life. Dr. Robbins just ordered me to cancel the show and I plan on refusing. I'm going through with it because my conscience will not permit retreat from black or any other kind of anti-Semitism. I'm fully prepared to commit insubordination. I may even lose my job in the end. Now there's the comic part. Because of Jews I'm going to possibly wreck my career."

At that moment Amelia Brown passed, obviously pleased to see us on speaking terms. Mitch broke away and with a wild light in his eyes shouted to Amelia, "Did you hear that, Mrs. Brown, did you hear that? He just said that his career was going to be wrecked by the Jews. Now can you believe that he's an anti-Semite?"

"Mitch, Mitch," I tried to interrupt. "You did it again. You're quoting me out of context."

"Did you or did you not say the Jews were going to wreck your career?" he shouted.

"Of course I said it, you twit, three seconds ago. But I said some other things before and after it."

"But you said it. You said it!"

The situation was ridiculous. Full of good feelings, I laughed. "Mitch, I'd love to continue fun and games with your impressive logic but I have a class waiting upstairs."

Amelia's point had been made. Mitch was acting irrationally and emotionally. I was pleased to have had Amelia, an assistant principal, see the desperation in the opposition's tactics; and Mitch, of course, had another story to tell proving my anti-Semitism.

These recollections were momentarily forgotten as my mind wandered back to the performance of the showcase segment of *Fiddler*. Most of the children were superb. Teddy Smith, as I feared, pushed Tevye's character aside and gave a totally undisciplined standup comic's routine. The audiences squealed with glee and marched out of the auditorium singing "Tradition." Some teachers voiced their distress over the children's hall-singing, and once the youngsters realized it was annoying, they sang simply to incite confrontation.

It was disappointing to learn later that several members of the opposition chose to remain in the faculty room drinking coffee rather than come to the auditorium to judge for themselves the style and tone of the performers. Some commented reluctantly on the rightness of the children's portrayals of Motel, Avram, Yente, and Golde. Bernice Rosen found Olga Carter's Yente offensive. I assured her that Olga was conscientiously searching for characterization and would have to be toned down when she found it. No teacher could have failed to grasp the point that after only four days of stage rehearsals these children had presented a near-perfect segment of the show. It was obvious that their work during the strike was serious. The cast was flushed with excitement at audience responses to their "Jewish things."

After the second assembly performance that Friday, I allowed excitement to grow in the prop room as the children removed their costumes and makeup. I cleared my throat and asked for attention.

"Gang, that was fantastic and I'm so proud of you I could burst. I'll save my notes for later but there is something I have to tell you."

They sensed danger and became silent.

"Please wait until I am through before you react," I continued. "I'm going to give it to you straight even though I promised Dr. Robbins I wouldn't. But I haven't thrown you any bullshit up to now and I don't intend to, ever. This show has been canceled. This is our last time doing it. *Crucible* tomorrow for good."

They were shocked and angry. When the noise subsided I went on.

"Most of you went through the *Oliver!* crisis and—"

"Those fucking Jews again," Duane exploded. "Why don't they leave us alone?"

Eileen declared, "I told you, Mr. Piro, that they wouldn't take this show without a fight."

Beverly was crying and said, "I don't think they have so much against *Fiddler,* Mr. Piro. I think they're just out to get you. Why?"

"Because, Bev," I answered, "certain teachers sit around all day crabbing about how stupid and uncooperative the kids in this school are. Then they see a fantastic Shakespeare or Molière production presented by these same so-called stupid kids. It shows them up for what they really are, ineffective teachers. No one likes to be shown up. They say you cannot learn. You prove you can. They take it out on me for letting you prove your point."

Teddy added, "We were supposed to have a science test this period, right? So I asked the teacher if I could take a makeup because I had to be here for the show. He says, 'If you want to waste your time with Mr. Piro, you'll just have to fail science.' Do you think that's fair?"

"Teddy, it's not only not fair but it's illegal since you all had the principal's written permission to be absent from science. I'll take it up with him. Hey, gang, if at any time you feel that you are not receiving proper grades because of your work in drama please have your mothers call me."

By this time it was beginning to sink in that *Fiddler* was really over.

"The fact that no one has asked why this cancellation happened," I said, "gives me cause to believe that you already know why. But for the record let me tell you that certain teachers fear the reaction of community leaders to a Jewish play. Until Dr. Robbins has written consent from these leaders we have to stop. I'm not going to mention any specific teacher so don't bother to ask."

The children didn't ask. They started reciting the list of teachers who had been vocal in their classes against the show.

"Mr. Piro," Maritza said, "what are we going to do now?"

"We're going back to *The Crucible* and pick up the third act right where we left it."

There was more commotion since certain students who had leads in *Fiddler* did not have comparable parts in *Crucible*. Maritza was one of them. She remained silent. During the din I left the children unsupervised. They needed time to formulate their own thoughts without adult interference.

After lunch I taught a large General Music class. They came to order and I focused on a boy who had failed to remove his hat in the classroom—a common occurrence. (Often a hat in class covered up a bad haircut given by a parent who could not afford a barber.) I took a chance and said, "Would you please remove your hat? What are you, a Jew or something?"

As expected, there was instant laughter. A black child had been "accused" of being a Jew by a teacher. The class slapped their legs in ridicule. No matter that the victim of their jeering was a classmate.

The boy quickly reached up to remove the hat, but stopped and merely adjusted the angle of the brim.

"Why'd you have to say that, Mr. Piro?" he asked, sullenly.

"Say what?" I questioned.

"About bein' a Jew."

I pretended embarrassment.

"Oh, well," I groped, "I mean that Jews wear hats indoors and at weddings and funerals and in their religion it's considered bad not to wear a hat. They even eat company dinners with hats on."

"No you didn't," he contradicted. "You said it like it was bad or something. Bein' a Jew ain't bad. It's just like bein' colored. You can't help the way you was born."

There was loud class agreement. This was one of the grades who had seen that morning's production in assembly. I needed the story at that moment. It was a small thing, granted, but it could grow.

That evening Mrs. Lillian Carter, mother of our Yente, called me at home. Lil Carter was a militant black woman who worked from inside the schools. She resisted all establishment attempts to enlist her considerable organizational powers in official capacities such as PTA presidencies or other parent-action groups. She knew her major effect was as a free agent and troubleshooter and understood what happened when parents became part of the establishment, especially in schools. She had been heard to boast, "I've broken three principals in my district." As a result she was a force some of us feared.

"Mr. Piro. Olga came home from school today and was very upset that you canceled *Fiddler*. She seems confused as to why and I thought you could help me to understand what's going on."

I gave her the story as straight as I could, leaving out no name, date, teacher, or detail.

"Wait a minute," she said. "You're talking about Jews and

the community and anti-Semitism. I don't care about all that. What I want to know is this. It wasn't easy for me or any mother to send our children to Manhattan every day. Now you tell me that it's all over. Why was it good then and not now?" (I thought, Dr. Robbins will never believe I didn't set this one up.)

Lil Carter knew the ramifications of the situation but was playing it cool. She suggested that I call Mrs. Frances Brown, leader in school affairs through the Brownsville Community Council.

"Mr. Piro," Lil commanded, "this is the woman you need. Be straight with her and you'll be amazed at what she can do and how fast she can do it. Call her at home any time. Listen, now. Trust her, y'hear?"

A Federally funded antipoverty agency, the Brownsville Community Council was run by officers elected by the community. With some trepidation at ignoring the traditional bureaucratic chain of command, I went outside the educational system and called Frances Brown, an important figure on the Council. She had a reputation for possessing a sharp mind and would tolerate no nonsense from teachers, parents, or students. I reviewed the events before making the call. Here was a woman that I could not charm, and contact with her meant I was involving an organization which carried considerable power in the community.

Frances Brown answered the phone. I needed neither explanation nor apology for calling outside of business hours. She had been personally interested in the outcome of the *Fiddler* situation and had been kept apprised of events as they happened through an intricate system of personal contacts. She had been waiting for my SOS. Her response was characteristically brief.

"Mr. Piro," she said. "You will do *Fiddler on the Roof* exactly as you planned it. This is a promise. Yes. I guarantee it."

"Aren't you underestimating Jewish power?" I asked.

"Mr. Piro, I said I promised and I don't often promise that which I can't deliver."

She then suggested that I set up a meeting for a faculty-community confrontation to which she would bring those leaders who were capable of officially assuring Dr. Robbins that the production would engender no racial reprisals.

The next morning I dutifully informed Robbins of the conversations and, since he trusted Frances Brown, he gave "temporary" permission for the resumption of *Fiddler* rehearsals. Community control of the schools was becoming a reality and he welcomed any opportunity to have parents make staff decisions. He had little to lose in exploring this newest crisis. My focus was on keeping the show alive. I thought of each day, step by step, but lacked the courage to consider the outcome seriously. This was the first of several cancellations. In the prop room there were two shopping bags, one with *Fiddler* scripts and the other with *The Crucible*. Rehearsals fluctuated between the two depending upon reactions from the community, faculty, and Robbins. What displeased me was the fact that Arthur Miller's great drama about the Salem witch-hunts had become second fiddle to *Fiddler* in the minds of the children. *The Crucible* deserved a better classification.

These events happened between the middle and end of November. I set Christmas vacation as a deadline. If we could not go ahead full steam on *Fiddler* by the second day of January, we would have to throw our full resources into *The Crucible*. I doubt the situation would ever come to that. It was a fool's doubt.

7

The community-staff meeting was set for the following Wednesday morning at ten o'clock. Amelia Brown handled parent notification and saw to it that I was officially relieved of teaching duties for the duration of the conference. Just before 10 A.M. I went to the office expecting to greet parents as they arrived. The large table at the far end of the room was prepared with ashtrays, note pads, and about twelve chairs. Dr. Robbins was not there. Amelia was sitting at his desk speaking on the telephone. She saw my concern and said, "Dick, Dr. Robbins will not be in today. He's ill. He asked me to chair the meeting."

I left the office. Bruce passed by and saw my frown.

"What's the matter?" he asked.

"Robbins isn't coming in today. Amelia's taking over."

"That's great," he exclaimed. "I've been racking my brain on how to record the meeting for Howard Enders without exterior microphones. Now I won't have to. Since Robbins is out, why don't we just set a machine on the table and tell the people that we want to give him an exact recording? Then instead of telling him what happened, we'll just hand him a tape."

"Bruce, you're fantastic. Do you know what a phoenix is?"

"Screw you," he laughed, delighted with himself, and moved into the sound-control room next to the office to set up the equipment. I noticed Mrs. Grayman hurrying down the hall towards the office. She was a small, darting black woman, one of three area workers assigned to our school by the Brownsville Community Council. Her duties consisted of assisting the school through home visits. In communicating with the professional staff most parents were inhibited by what they considered their lack of sophisticated vocabulary and grammar. Mrs. Grayman was not. She introduced major arguments with, "I's gonna tell it just like it is." And did. We chatted about everything except *Fiddler on the Roof*. Since she knew the nature of the meeting, I took this as indication of support.

A few minutes later we were joined by Mrs. Diaz, her Puerto Rican counterpart. Where Mrs. Grayman lashed out with machine-gun force, Mrs. Diaz, whose command of English was apparently limited, remained silent at racially mixed meetings. She watched, perceived, and, when necessary, spoke with careful precision and a heavy Spanish accent. Grayman attacked. Diaz defended. Both women served their respective communities with dedication and dignity, enjoying the respect of the community and the school. We left the doorway and entered the office. Amelia was still on the phone. I ushered the ladies to seats and then nervously rearranged the ashtrays and pads on the table. Much depended on this meeting. Frances Brown had promised delivery of the top power structure. Where were they? Bruce then entered with the tape recorder and took over the pleasantries.

Larry Franklyn, our union chapter chairman, passed by and, after I briefly explained what was happening, decided to join us out of curiosity. He had guided our chapter through the strike and I was pleased with the cordiality of Mrs. Grayman's and Mrs. Diaz's greetings. It was then twenty minutes past the announced starting time.

Suddenly the door was filled with the awesome presence of Mrs. Lillian Carter, my leading parent supporter. She ignored my gushing welcome and cast a firm eye around the room, noting who was absent with obvious displeasure. Lil was a big woman representing a solid mass of defined force. What she set out to do she did. She was deliberate, articulate, well informed, and fed up with inefficiency. Having been active in several schools, she was professional enough to realize that within a single neighborhood, school standards varied from excellent to unacceptable. Our school was her showcase example. Though her daughter, Olga, was playing Yente in *Fiddler,* I had no doubt that she was primarily concerned with larger issues beyond the wish to see her child featured on stage. She walked slowly into the room, nodding to Amelia and the other ladies.

Mrs. Diaz was the first one to note the microphones on the table. A glance was passed to Mrs. Grayman. I waited. Nothing was said. Amelia finished her calls and took her seat at the head of the table, announcing Dr. Robbins' absence. At that moment Frances Brown, representative of the Brownsville Community Council, swiftly entered and took a seat while apologizing for the absence of the other community leaders. A public-housing crisis had come up, she explained. They promised to come later if possible. Frances Brown was obviously upset but this was small comfort to my own disappointment. We settled around the table. I stood off to the side in order to monitor the tape.

This was my first face-to-face experience with Frances Brown and I was anticipating some fireworks. She was a stunning woman, elegantly but simply dressed in a beige linen suit with a dark brown felt hat sitting jauntily at the back of her head. She projected warmth, charm, openness, poise, and a sense of being coiled. She demanded performance and through sheer ability was quickly rising to the top of the neighborhood power structure through the Brownsville Community Council. With people like Frances Brown ready for service, decentralization of schools wasn't the specter some teachers considered it.

My glance swept the table. The group was small but represented a good cross section of attitudes: Grayman—blitz; Diaz—defense; Carter—battering ram; Amelia Brown—traditional manipulation; Larry Franklyn—curiosity; Bruce Birnel—caution; and Frances Brown—efficiency. I had no intention of participating in the discussion. My position as sponsor of the project was clear. I was present to listen and monitor recording levels.

Amelia began, "By now you've all noticed that we intend to tape this discussion so that Dr. Robbins will be able to listen to it later. Are there any objections?"

"Not me," Frances Brown said. "If I'm going to be quoted I'd just as soon be quoted exactly. Tape away."

Amelia raised her normally pleasant voice to chairlady shrillness and asked me if I would provide the group with background. I rose and gave a chronological sequence of events, stating the justification of the show.

Towards the end of my account, Amelia interrupted. "It was Dr. Robbins' feeling," she said, "that perhaps the community would want something that would really provide positive identification for the pupils. Perhaps something Afro-American or something Puerto Rican. And there are some teachers, too, that expressed this feeling. Perhaps the idea of retaining one's identity would be better expressed by some other play."

Frances Brown immediately objected to Amelia's intrusion. "Mrs. Brown," she scolded, "Mr. Piro has not finished his statement and you have interrupted it already. Let's have a one-to-one, and then go down the line."

Amelia was hurt. She was not going to be able to manipulate this discussion, an art she had spent fifteen years developing.

Mrs. Grayman spoke next. She admitted to having had a private discussion with Dr. Robbins the previous day. It was her feeling that the Jewish staff were attempting to hide the similarities of their assimilation problems to those experienced by blacks.

"I mean," she said, "Jews have been poor, and they have lived in the ghettos, and this is what we blacks are doing right now. I thought this project was a wonderful idea because it would give the children a chance to realize that there is a way out for us. The children tend to think that because we're black we're *supposed* to be poor."

There was vocal approval of her statement. It was the clue Amelia had needed. She said, "Well, this is exactly the way I felt. I think that if the community wanted it then I consider it done."

Frances Brown looked up and noted with irritation Amelia's willingness to go with the strength.

There we were—nowhere. The parents were for the play. Amelia was for the parents. The president and executive board of the Brownsville Community Council were not present. Further discussion was pointless.

"Mrs. Brown," I said, "the leading member of the faculty group opposing *Fiddler* is teaching a class right now but will be free in five minutes. Why don't I go up and offer to relieve him of his next class so that he can come down here and present his views?"

Amelia agreed and I went to get Mitchell Grossman. Together we returned to the meeting. I indicated a seat at the end of the table, opposite Amelia Brown and next to Mrs. Frances Brown. I glanced at Mitch to inform him that the meeting was being recorded.

The ladies observed Mitch with curiosity. Without

waiting to be introduced he began, "I would like to voice an objection to this discussion."

The friendly atmosphere subtly turned to hostility. The women were not reacting to words as much as to a patronizing manner. Mitch's vocabulary was adjusted to peers, but his attitude and tone of voice seemed to indicate their inferiority.

"I'm quite active in Jewish affairs," he went on. "In this time of tension when anti-Semitism is very, very high, I feel that the presentation of *Fiddler* would be unwise because it would be playing into certain anti-Semitic feelings. I pick up the *Times* every day and I read in the paper about the serious hatred.

"Now I'm in total empathy with the struggles and trials of the Negro community. But, as a Jew, I am rather sensitive to the presentation of *Fiddler.* Not only that the director of *Fiddler,* a man whom I respect for his talents—Mr. Piro—has voiced to me many anti-Semitic remarks, but I feel his direction would encourage a lot of anti-Semitic feelings with the children. I don't think the universal message of the play will get across as he will present it. When he has kids dancing around with sacred Jewish garments, skullcaps, and whatnot, I think it will prove to be quite offensive."

He paused for breath. Amelia looked at the closed faces around the table and said, "I think we ought to react at this time."

Lil Carter asked, "Mr. Grossman, did you see *Fiddler* on Broadway?"

"Twice," he said, proudly.

"Why didn't you object to it on Broadway?" she asked.

"Well, Broadway, you see, is something else," Mitch said. "A man goes to Broadway because he wants to see a production for *x* amount of dollars. I feel a production of *Fiddler* on a very local level will be feeding into—playing into—a lot of anti-Semitic feelings. Broadway is different."

Frances Brown uncoiled and angrily interjected, "No, I'm sorry. It's the same thing I said before. You're telling us that the quality of the people seeing our shows in Brownsville is not the same as those persons who go up to Broadway. Therefore, their way of responding is definitely different than the way that it may be responded to here."

Mitch instantly grasped her point and tried to reword his thought but couldn't be heard above the din of approval from the ladies. Frances Brown called out, "I'm saying exactly what was said, Mr. Grossman, because in your remarks you did not say it openly, so I did."

Regaining the group's attention, Mitch then related my failure to answer his question about the Nazi Party convention. His story brought silence to the room. After a pause Frances Brown asked quietly, "Are you aware, Mr. Grossman, that this play is being put on all over the city right now?"

"It is being performed on Broadway."

"You're not answering me," she shot out. "I'm saying that there are anti-Semitic feelings at this time throughout the city and, consequently, would you recommend that, because of anti-Semitic feelings throughout the city you would object to and stop productions of *Fiddler*? I would then have to ask you if you felt that if it were put on in the proper manner—and I'm not saying taking so much out of it that it no longer looks like *Fiddler on the Roof*—would you then feel differently about that?"

"Well," Mitch said uncomfortably, "I still feel that a production would be inappropriate."

These parents had experienced Frances Brown in action. We of the staff had not.

"What part or portion of the play do you find objectionable?" she asked.

"Well, first of all, the wearing of the Jewish religious garb. I feel this would be a—"

"By non-Jews?"

"No. Yes, by non-Jews. In local areas. *Local* areas."

"I don't understand you," she said with a hint of impatience.

"Well, I pick up *The New York Times* every day and I read that there is a tremendous amount of anti-Semitism."

"There always has been!"

"Yes. But now it is coming to a head. It is spreading even more."

"You're not answering my question, Mr. Grossman. You started to answer—the garments—and you feel that these garments will be worn by non-Jews. So wherever this play is being put on throughout the city—"

Mitch saw the direction of her argument and hesitated with, "No. I—"

"Well, I want clarity," Frances Brown demanded. "If I'm not speaking from clarity I cannot properly state my views."

Mitch then attempted a change of the direction of the discussion by shouting, "The man who is producing the show is an anti-Semite because he has made anti-Semitic remarks to me."

His outburst was met by cold silence. Lil Carter broke the hush. "If Mrs. Amelia Brown were putting on the show would you object?" she asked.

"No."

"I didn't think so." Lil sat back, content with her point. Now that Frances Brown had set up the lines of attack, Mrs. Grayman said, "I'm not much for a lot of fancy words, but I feel now that the main point seems to be this. You could probably put it in a more educated way, but to my thinking this teacher don't want to see no black child—"

"No. No. No," Mitch objected. "You're reading into it. I think a black child could play it. It all depends upon the director."

Everyone began talking at once. Amelia brought the meeting to order. "Is there anything else you would like to say, Mr. Grossman?"

"Why this tremendous urge to produce *Fiddler on the Roof*?" he asked.

"I'll tell you my reason why," Lil Carter said. "Ever since before I was hatched, the white man was playing Negro. They blacked their faces. They wore our clothes and were entertaining people by imitating us and making fun of the way we spoke, we walked, and we sang. And who was there to object? Nobody."

Frances Brown held up her hand to stop Mitch's objection, and said, "At this point I must say that I grew up in a Jewish neighborhood."

"And some of your best friends are Jews?" Mitch smiled.

"No! Don't you put words in my mouth." She paused and glared at him. "And in growing up in a Jewish neighborhood, where my father was a janitor in the house, I went through what you're worrying about—what you've gone through. But at the same time, it helped me to develop. Many of the boys and girls in this school only know you because you are the teacher who comes to them. They do not know Jews as neighbors. I do. I know you as a neighbor because I grew up in the atmosphere of your people. Therefore, I see you differently. I get the impression that you're worried the children may see you differently.

"Neighborhoods are changing with people running from one another," she continued. "The average human being seldom knows other human beings. The situation here can bring awareness."

Amelia Brown gathered her notes together, the traditional signal for dismissal. "May I say, Mr. Grossman, in every situation each person should have the courage to be either for or against. This is a democracy. Remember, before the election we are Democrats or Republicans but after the election we are all Americans." Amelia started to rise.

Frances Brown was not quite ready for dismissal. "May I ask Mr. Grossman one thing?" she asked. "This particular situation has reached the point where the boiling is about to break the pot. I personally would hope to see that the heat under this pot is not turned up by you or any other teacher. You control the level of that heat."

"Well, I said—" Mitch began.

"Let's not confuse these kids any more. Now, all I'm saying is that as far as this play is concerned, I would hope that it will not be watered down to a level where we no longer recognize it as *Fiddler on the Roof.*"

Amelia then summarized the discussion, and ended with her conviction that the community was receptive to the project. The group dispersed quickly. Mitch had gone through a humiliating experience. Several of his attempts to interrupt Amelia's summary failed. He was ignored. The meeting was over.

I helped Bruce pack up the equipment. We didn't have to speak.

The next day, I intercepted Dr. Robbins and joined him in his office while he checked his mail. I sat down by his desk, ready for a congratulatory message and permission to continue working on the show. He concentrated on opening the drawer to get an ashtray. Losing control, he suddenly slammed the drawer shut and hissed, "How could you permit Grossman to come down and humiliate this entire staff with his inanities? Amelia called me last night and I roasted her."

"Dr. Robbins," I said, stunned by his anger. "Have you listened to the tape?"

"No, and I don't intend to. I'm furious with her and furious with you. He's too dense to know any better but you and Amelia have worked with these people long enough to know in advance what Grossman was getting into. And you let it happen. What could you possibly have accomplished except to add another black eye to the staff?"

"Dr. Robbins," I said, "we don't use that expression any more."

"Damn it, I'm serious!"

"OK. So we made a mistake. Now can I go ahead full steam?"

"No."

"What do you mean, no? You said that—"

"I said, Mr. Piro, that if the president and executive board of the Brownsville Community Council gave me assurances there would be no reprisals for this show we would do it. Those people were not present, and you know it. Most of the people who did come have been in your pocket for years. They support Piro, period. That's not enough. Until I get what I want and until I get it in writing you'll go on with *The Crucible*."

He was right. I would have been surprised if his reaction had been different. It was a good try. Robbins agreed to call Frances Brown and inform her that he did not feel he had adequate expression of community support for *Fiddler*. I went to the auditorium for a rehearsal.

Teddy Smith came bounding in first.

"Which play we going to rehearse today, Mr. Piro, the Jews or the witches?"

"The witches."

"What? Wasn't the meeting going to clear up all that stuff? When I passed by the office yesterday, I peeked in. You were going strong."

"Not strong enough, Teddy. Would you just bring me the shopping bag with *Crucible* scripts so I can start the third-act cuts before the mob arrives? I'll explain the whole situation when everyone gets here. I don't want Beverly to see me with tears in my eyes."

"Those motherfuckin'—"

"Teddy, please. I've got something invested in this play,

too, and foul-mouthing the opposition isn't going to get us anywhere. Trust me. We're going to do *Fiddler*."

"But—"

The bell rang and the class flowed in carrying contraband sodas and ice cream from the lunch room. I waited. They saw the *Crucible* scripts spread over the edge of the stage and began the litany of curses.

"Come on, gang, knock it off," I said. "We held the meeting I had told you about but, as fate would have it, timing was off. There was some crisis in public housing. Therefore the 'proper' authorities were not able to attend and deliver the verdict to Dr. Robbins. I tried to bluff it through this morning but it just didn't work. He is very pissed off at me right now. After class I'm free if Duane decides to go on to his next class instead of trying to hide in the prop room with Tina. Then I'll call up Frances Brown and get to the next step of the campaign. So let's just go on as if nothing has happened, OK?"

The rehearsal went badly. Tempers were short and Teddy twice got involved in fights. *The Crucible* was turning into a kind of punishment and the children no longer took delight in the Salem witch-hunts of 1692. They also sensed my lack of interest in their work that day.

The children went on to their next class and I called Frances Brown and congratulated her on the brilliance of her presentation, finally relating that morning's conversation with Dr. Robbins. She was not surprised.

"He'll get what he wants, Mr. Piro. Trust me."

"That's exactly what I just told the kids—'trust me.' There's a lot of trust going on but very little action."

"He'll get what he wants. Give me two days."

After school the cast assembled in the prop room for news.

"Kids," I began, "I don't know about you but I've had it. I'm now going to ask you to give careful consideration to something that will require a vote from everyone. We have three plans and I need your help in choosing one. We can do the following: Either we go on rehearsing *Fiddler,* pretending nothing happened and—remember this—taking the real risk that we won't ever perform it. Or we can tell them all to go to hell and throw our strengths into *The Crucible.* Or we can drop both scripts and start on a third project. Any questions?"

There was the usual chaos engendered by any new idea thrown to a group of excited teen-agers. Children function as they see a film, frame by frame. My intent was to be impartial. I failed, then, as always, when relying on kids to make *my* decisions. It was a desperate fight against time. The on-again-off-again business was destroying both productions by making it impossible to begin building sets, designing costumes, and putting together a sound track. This behind-the-scenes work was still waiting, and without it the most talented cast cannot carry a production. The earlier theater successes rested largely on the fact that our shows were more exciting visually than anything many people had seen. This was not an accident, but a conscious decision Bruce and I had made three years before. Our easiest job was working with the children. Our most difficult assignments rested in those technical embellishments where we called upon our own standards of professionalism. Few schools had enough equipment, talent, imagination, and time to meet Broadway standards. We did. Yet, no one would miss what we were unwilling to do. It made the doing that much more difficult and, consequently, rewarding.

After some discussion, the children voted to "tell them to go to hell" and throw full resources into *The Crucible.* This vote was not pleasing, even though it would have been my choice. If the children had really desired *Crucible* I would have been overjoyed. As it was, they saw only the first frame of the proposal—"tell them to go to hell"—and voted unanimously.

"That I can tell you in one word—*tradition!*" Teddy Smith as Tevye instructs the audiences in the opening monologue of *Fiddler on the Roof*.

"Then you love me?" "I suppose I do." Beverly Cannon, as Golde, and Teddy affirm their love after twenty-five years of marriage. Below, Jew and Russian join in a celebration of a betrothal. Harold Moses, Steven Hirsch, Ronald Blanche, James Parker and Paul Marzan as the Rabbi.

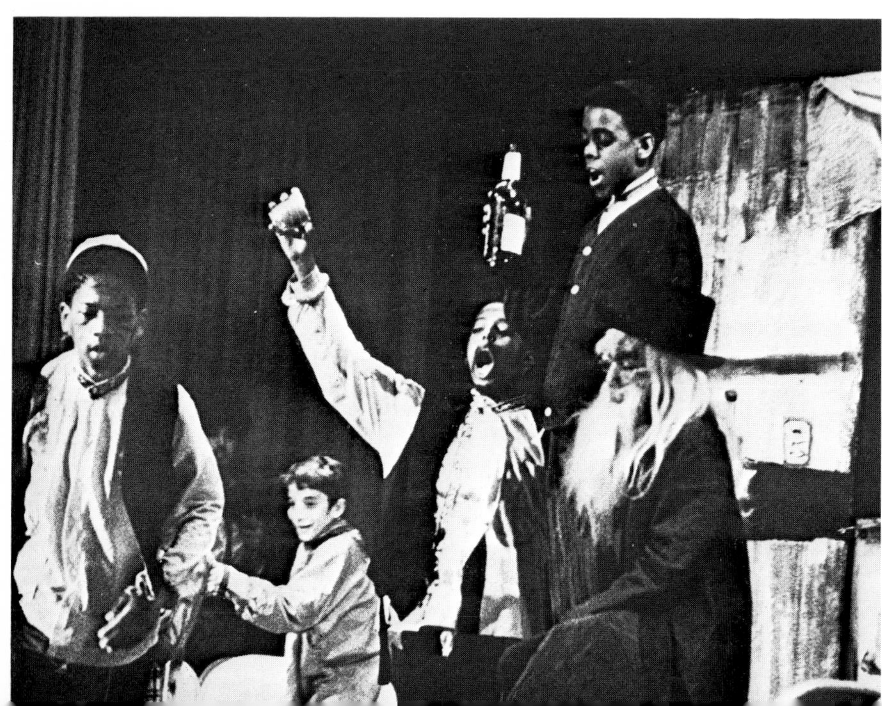

Hodel (Maritza Figuroa) and Chava (Sheila Haskins) ponder the possibilities of marriage as they sing "Matchmaker." Below, Tevye (Teddy Smith) converses with heaven. "Dear God, with your help I'm starving to death."

Tevye and Motel (Duane McCullers) rehearse Motel's announcement that he would be the perfect match for Tevye's daughter. Below, Shprintze (Diana Martinez) and Bielke (Carmen Ocasio) wait to be noticed on Sabbath Eve.

Sheila Haskins (Chava) and Linus Sellars (Fyedka) react as Piro insists that their bodies must touch from shoulder to heel.

Mary Collins, Teddy Smith, Sheila Haskins and Duane McCullers take a break during the ABC-TV filming of *Black Fiddler, The Negro and Prejudice.*

Loaded down with refreshments, Mary Collins, Olga Carter, Teddy Smith, Sharon Rutland and Terrance Raiford arrive at school for opening night. Below, opening night tension is obvious as Terrance Raiford, Beverly Cannon, Sheila Haskins, Steven Hirsch, Lolita Randolph and Jorge Pastor listen to Piro's intermission remarks.

A standing ovation on opening night brings relief and exuberance to cast and director as Tina Hardin leads the players in greeting Dick Piro for the last curtain call.

The group dispersed, unsure if they did the right thing and distrustful of my sudden swing to the democratic process.

I called after them. "Tonight I want everyone to light a candle to St. Frances in hope she can bring us the miracle we need." With not a Catholic in the group, the joke got no reaction. We drifted away, not angry, not disgusted, not hopeful, not excited, not depressed, not anything. And this was the worst state. The children were intimately familiar with it. I was not.

8

The next day the children slowly filed into drama class. To discourage questions, I turned my back and began stacking folding chairs left in the pit by the previous period's band rehearsal.

"Do you want some help?" Duane asked.

"Thanks, Duane, I'll do it. But you could get the props out and see that they're in the wings before we start."

"What props?" he said guardedly. "We didn't make any props for *The Crucible* yet—unless you mean . . ." A smile started at the corners of his mouth.

"Duane, don't blow it," I said quietly. "Hurry up. I want to talk for a minute before we begin rehearsing."

He stood in his tracks, torn between my request and his need for verification. Then, with untied sneaker laces flying, he ran into the prop room.

I hoisted myself on top of the spinet piano and asked for attention.

"Yesterday you all voted on something," I began. The children looked at each other nervously. "I'm not sure if I told you this or not, but I don't consider myself bound by your choice. I just can't let go of *Fiddler,* at least until the last avenue of approach has been exhausted. As I told you yesterday, I called Frances Brown and she asked for two days, maybe longer. It's the least we can give her. I also feel the primary force in your vote was to tell 'them' to go to hell. I asked myself, 'Why do we have to drop *Fiddler* in order to tell them to go to hell?' So I decided that the best way to thumb our noses at them was to go on as if they didn't exist. OK?"

The children let the words sink in and there was a moment's silence, rare for this group. Suddenly Teddy jumped up and said, "Hey Mr. Piro, do you know what *Fiddler on the Roof* is about?"

"No, Teddy, I don't. Maybe you'll tell us."

"Well, *Fiddler on the Roof* is about us trying to do *Fiddler on the Roof.*"

"What are you talking about?" Beverly demanded.

"I'm talking about being a Jew, Beverly."

The group heckled Teddy for being obscure. Getting angry, he leaped on the piano next to me and shouted, "Dig this, now. All of us in this cast are just like those Jews playing their fiddles on those roofs. Any minute we can fall on our asses and the show's over. And—get this—we can't do anything about it. So we just go on and on until we die."

Olga asked, "So what then, Teddy? What have we got except a little bit of this and a little bit of that?"

The group giggled at Olga's quote from the "Anatevka" lyric.

"Wait a minute, Olga," Teddy responded. "You know what we've got?" He smiled enigmatically.

"What?"

"We've got a nice song." Pleased with his thought, Teddy moved off the piano and on to the stage.

I shouted in cheerleader fashion, "Who's a Jew?"

"We're a Jew," the group responded in unison.

"What have we got?" I shouted.

"We've got *Fiddler on the Roof,*" they screamed.

"OK," I said. "Let's get our Jewish behinds on that stage and do the best damn wedding-reception scene the world has ever seen."

Gleefully the cast marched on stage, took positions, and began work resulting in a superb rehearsal-performance. This spirit lasted for the next few days, and I anticipated a wild Friday windup.

Rehearsal scheduling was arranged so that individual progress reached a peak on Friday after school. Often this was the first opportunity the company had of seeing certain solo bits that had been polished privately during times snatched away from the week. It was understood by students that if I saw a cast member out of class during one of my free periods, he was "kidnaped" and made to work on the show. The children's lunch periods were always up for grabs. Any scene involving physical contact in a romantic situation was rehearsed in privacy until the actors had lost all sense of embarrassment. It was then shown for viewing on Friday afternoon's runthrough. These stolen moments were the foundation of some children's work, and we all looked forward to Friday's revelations.

That Friday morning, Bruce presented a typical ultimatum.

"If you want lights hung," he demanded, "I must have the exact location of every piece of scenery. I want this marked on the stage floor with different colors of masking tape. I've cleared this afternoon with my other job and we're going to talk lights."

"Friday, Bruce? It has to be today?" I pleaded.

"If I can't do it today I don't know when I can," he insisted.

Another squeeze. We had finally lost the fervor of Teddy's "Jewish Declaration" and rehearsal the day before had gone badly. We all needed the Friday push to keep spirits alive through the weekend. I was also hesitant about taking this giant step with Bruce and the lights. It was a major undertaking and we still lacked permission to go for score.

During the in-school drama period I spoke of the conflict and explained the enormity of the technical tasks yet to be done on the show. "Therefore," I concluded, "I deeply regret that I have to meet with Mr. Birnel after school so we can't rehearse."

The children cheered the cancellation announcement. The ensuing rehearsal was as bad as the previous day's. I lost my temper. As usual Teddy and I flung insults at each other. In disgust I left the auditorium a few minutes before the bell rang.

After school I went into the empty auditorium to wait for Bruce. I thought, So much has happened since the last moment of introspection following the *Oliver!* close. I sensed Bruce's presence in the darkness a few rows behind me. What were his personal investments in *Fiddler*? I related each new pressure incident to him as a story happening to an interested observer. His help on strategy was given more as a lawyer than as a defendant. His trust hurt because along with the children, Bruce, too, had to have had feelings at stake. This unconditional faith in my ability to see us through was intimidating. I loved him for it.

"Hey," Bruce said, suddenly breaking the mood, "I think I've got a solution to the Sabbath Prayer set. Don't say a word. Do as I ask and then go out front and look."

He bounded on the stage. Together we began stacking rectangular lunchroom tables one on top of the other against the back wall. I had no idea what his plan was but, since it kept me busy, I went along, never observing a frame larger than my immediate vision. I heard a pounding on the side door and went to investigate. It was Teddy and Duane.

"You do know," I said, "there's no rehearsal today, don't you?"

"Yeah, we know." They glanced past me to the stage and noted Bruce's excitement.

"Well, you're welcome to stay but Mr. Birnel and I are going to be working, so no noise. OK?"

"All right."

The boys went into the house and sat down. I continued placing tables and chairs at Bruce's direction. Finally, he ordered me to leave the stage and go into the totally dark house. Gingerly I found a path through the music stands in the pit and took a seat in the middle of the auditorium. Bruce threw some light switches and lo, we had our Sabbath Prayer scene, including two transparent gauze scrims to duplicate—and even improve upon—the effect of the Broadway production.

"Bruce," I shouted, overjoyed, "that's incredible." Then the teacher-in-the-director noticed the dangers involved with heavy stacked tables and crawling, excited teen-agers. Bruce came out to join me in the adulation of his creation.

"How are the kids going to get to the top level?" I asked.

"I don't know," he beamed. "We'll climb that bridge when we come to it."

He left, adjusted light levels, and then returned to the seats.

"My problem is this," he started. I tuned out. The technical problems of getting enough light in the proper places did not hold the same fascination for me as they did for Bruce. My interest lay in results, not process. While he shared his thinking of each step of the scene, I looked and enjoyed the visual effect he had created while delighting in my good fortune at having him on the team. Evidently he realized my lack of attention, got up abruptly, and turned on the house lights. Hearing a gasp, I turned and looked towards the back rows. Most of the cast had joined Teddy and Duane and were sitting quietly, observing our excitement. As silently as they had entered they filtered out. Only Duane said good-

was to round up the cast with Bruce and spread the word. The intention lasted as long as it took to cross the street. Bruce passed the main entrance of school as I reentered the building.

"Where were you?" he asked.

Without a word I took his arm and steered him to the privacy of the prop room.

"Bruce," I began, "I'm in a big rush so please don't ask questions. We're going to do the show. Frances Brown just told me the letter from the Brownsville Community Council has been sent. It should be here tomorrow."

"But that's terrific! What are you so breathless about?"

"Never mind. I'm going to type a letter informing the world that we have shifted over to *The Crucible* as our spring major show."

"But now that *Fiddler* has been cleared—"

"I told you, Bruce, and you didn't listen. We *are* going to do *Fiddler*."

"So what's with a letter about *Crucible*?"

"Evil, Bruce. Pure evil. Frances Brown's clearance will arrive tomorrow. My announcement will be made today."

"Hey. I'm reading you." His eyes twinkled with the idea.

Looking persecuted I entered the general office. The secretaries noted my depression and appeared sympathetic. Amelia Brown winked encouragement as she walked into a conference with Dr. Robbins. Finding a free typewriter, I made a stencil of the following memo:

TO: Drama Class
FROM: R. J. Piro
SUBJECT: Casting of The Crucible and Other Things

The following cast is announced pending behavior and talent problems. After a week we will cast understudies and replacements for the attached characters. It's nag time: We have an incredible amount of time to make up. It will be, again, making history with this play. It is the first full four-act drama (without music) that has ever been performed at this school. It is also one of the greatest (American) dramas ever written. It is also my favorite play of all time. It is also by Arthur Miller, a living, still working author. (I can't spell the type of author who writes only plays.)

I WILL NOT TOLERATE ANY SORT OF NONSENSE DURING OUR REHEARSAL TIMES BOTH DURING AND AFTER SCHOOL!!!! This play calls for a big cast and there will be lots of times when you will be sitting in the audience as we work with small character scenes. I promise you I will be vicious when distracted by your conversations. We have lots of room for you in our school chorus and Mr. Birnel will be glad to accept you. If you are unwilling to make this deal right now—to sit quietly and either listen or do your homework or read or study lines—then it will be better for all of us if you left now and we could replace you immediately with no hard feelings.

We have all been victims of circumstance and now, being troupers, it is our job to make up lost time—simply because we are good enough to do a fantastic piece of theater REGARDLESS of adult hangups. I am VERY excited about this project. It has become my total self. How about you?

Love from the Monster-That-Is but
soon to become the Monster-That-Was

Quickly I placed mimeographed copies of this letter in the boxes of Dr. Robbins, all supervisors, and friends of the cast, including those who had appeared to be friends but who had been reporting each of my lunchroom conversations back to the opposition. These "spies" had one last planted rumor to spread. Since Teddy had helped me work the mimeograph machine, I was certain a number of copies would find their way into the cast's hands within the hour. On Mondays we had no rehearsals scheduled, which eliminated the possibility of further explanations.

At the end of the day I purposely ran into Dr. Robbins and put a bit of extra bounce into my greeting. He murmured words such as "flexibility" and "glad to see no hard feelings are being transmitted to the kids." It was evil. I knew and savored it. Now I could afford indulgence in feelings. The "victory announcement" was but a few hours away.

The next morning at 11 A.M. Dr. Robbins' secretary asked if I would see him. I entered the office, lit a cigarette and babbled on about how great *Crucible* was going to be and the tremendous relevance of this show at this time, especially following the aborted *Fiddler* attempt.

"You don't look excited, Dr. Robbins," I said.

"I'm not," he replied. "I'm simply embarrassed. I've been in this crazy business too long to take much personally, but I confess to being very embarrassed—and sorry. I read your memo to the kids. I was proud of you and them but especially you. You'll last a long time in this education game. But I'm afraid I have bad news."

"Bad news? Is there an Association of Salem Witches who're having their sensitivities offended now?"

He avoided the wisecrack and said, "I'm afraid I'm going to have to require you to put *Fiddler* back on the boards."

"What?"

"I just got this letter. Read it."

He placed the letter in my hand and turned to look out the window. I opened the envelope.

Brownsville Community Council

Dear Dr. Robbins:

We urgently request that Junior High School 275 be allowed to put on the Fiddler on the Roof play. The performing arts know no boundary of race. Therefore this play, as an experience dealing with Jewish culture, can be a great enlightenment to the black and Puerto Rican youth of Brownsville, especially as staged by black and Puerto Rican students.

Yours respectfully,

It was signed by the president of the Council and co-signed by the board of directors. Frances Brown had delivered.

Robbins turned for my reaction. Here was the moment. I let it pass, not having the courage to tell him I faked the *Crucible* business to heighten his embarrassment. However I lacked sufficient gall to continue the dishonesty. Intuition told me that he was genuinely excited and knowledge of my deceit might have weakened his support. Thus, where he had expected a typical Piro tirade, he was shocked by a simple, "OK, Dr. Robbins. We go for score starting this afternoon."

I rose to leave, anxious to spread the good news. He stopped me.

"You know, Dick, the teachers are not going to like this and they're going to howl. But, damn it, I'm running a school *for* this community and that community is going to get what they want so long as it is in my power to give it to them. I don't know how you do it but everything you touch turns to gold. So I'm going to call an informal meeting of all teachers next Monday and give them a chance to hash this out officially. It's the least we can do. Sensitivities have been offended. I have absolute trust in your ability to produce this show in the best of taste. Would you care to set up the meeting?"

Leaving his office, I typed up a notice informing the staff of a discussion-meeting of all interested parties concerning the forthcoming production of *Fiddler on the Roof* and posted it over the time clock.

Within the hour, the children greeted the news with a near-riot. The cast poured onto the stage, everyone anxious to imitate his favorite character. Teddy decided to play the Russian Constable and George (the real Constable) played Teddy with a heavy Colombian accent. We were nearly destroyed with laughter. Beverly chose to do a "soul Yente" and began the scene with, "Petunia, dahlin', ah has such news it goin' to bust yo' tits."

Little was accomplished in terms of opening-night preparation but we did have an exciting two days of celebrating. Bruce attacked the technical problems with abandon and remained after school until late that evening hanging the first set of lights.

Two days later, on Thursday, Abe Gron, our newly elected union chapter chairman, suggested that since he had done a meticulous job of mending wounded sensitivities, there was no longer any need for a staff meeting. "All parties," he said, "had decided to withdraw active opposition if I would agree to a Watchdog Committee insuring that no further offense would be given." I related these facts to Dr. Robbins and he agreed to cancel the session.

The next day, as I was eating lunch, the door was thrown open and Aaron Marcus, a towering six-foot-tall history teacher, strode over to my table, followed by several other male teachers.

"Just one thing, Piro," he boomed. "Are you or are you not going to go through with *Fiddler on the Roof*?" Crumpled in his hand was one of the *Crucible* casting memos.

I looked up, shocked at the threatening tone and embarrassed both for him and myself.

"Yes," I said, calmly as possible.

"Oh no you're not," he shouted. "Because we're going to *destroy* you. You've had your chance to back off but now when we're through with you you'll never get another job anywhere in the country." His chest was heaving with fury and his words interrupted with great gulps of breath. The room became silent as more than fifty teachers paused in their eating.

"We're going to expose your personal life through detectives," he continued, "and then publish the results in *The New York Times*. We're going to reveal the real reason why you were fired from Scarsdale. We'll get you everywhere you turn."

Still trying to appear calm but really frightened that the situation might end in physical violence, I said, "Aaron, my Scarsdale file is intact and with Dr. Robbins. We'll be glad to lend it to you so you can be sure of your factual material before you begin."

In frustration he threw over some chairs, but further violence was thwarted by his friends, who hurried him out of the room. I waited for reactions. The room quickly returned to normal. Not one word of encouragement. Not one word of criticism of this type of behavior. It was my turn to be shocked. A moment later Mimi Winston, an English teacher who supported our project, joined me.

"What happened?" she asked, "I just saw Mr. Marcus storming into Dr. Robbins' office." She patiently listened to my reactions with silent sympathy.

Over the weekend I thought about the concept of a Watchdog Committee (a term Abe Gron wished to avoid). By Sunday I was so upset I wrote and distributed a letter to Abe, Dr. Robbins, and selected members of the Watchdog Committee. The memo proved unnecessary. Opposition members refused to sit on a Watchdog Committee. They reasoned that participation on such a committee represented approval of our *Fiddler* production, and this was precisely what they wished to avoid.

That afternoon I retreated to the prop room for a double period of costume inventory. It was here that Bernice Rosen, still my friend, came to find me.

"Dick?"

"Bunny. Come in."

"Thanks, but I'm going across the street for coffee. Will you come?"

"Sure. But let me wind up here first. You go on and get a table and I'll be there in a few minutes."

Finished, I walked slowly over to the restaurant. Something was brewing. Bunny was opposition, articulate and militant. Hardly a day had gone by, before the controversy, when we did not share a cup of coffee and bask in the radiance of our mutual respect and affection. Bernice gave the outward appearance of being a typical buxom, matronly Jewish mother with two daughters in high school. It was not so. Although devoted to her husband and children, she was keenly aware of her own needs. After her children had reached puberty she began college, earned her degrees, and with full credentials began a teaching career. With this goal realized she continued taking evening courses. We spent many a free period discussing Shelley, Keats, Bryon, Opera, Police Tactics, Seventeenth-Century Drama, or whatever else she was currently studying. She worked hard and the students respected and liked her. Several graduates of our school entered colleges to pursue teaching careers because of their experiences with Mrs. Rosen. Each time I invited guests in to observe our school, I insisted they spend a period observing Bernice in action. There is no higher compliment I could give her. She took pleasure in this professional adulation of her work. In spite of the difference in our ages—she a middle-aged mother of three teen-age daughters, and I a bachelor in my early thirties—there was an element of romance in our relationship. My response to her was to a total woman, charming, intelligent, witty, warm, and attractive. I missed our kaffeeklatches in the past few weeks. We had been avoiding each other, knowing the impossibility of not talking about *Fiddler*. We treasured our friendship and were reluctant to risk a break over the controversy.

"Dick, I want to talk about *Fiddler,*" she said nervously as I slid into the booth. I was so happy to be with her that I held back the usual defensive remarks.

"OK, so talk," I said. "And I promise I won't be swayed by what you say because of my love for you."

This remark was unfair and it shook her. She began haltingly. "Do you know why so many teachers are against this show?"

"I think so, but why don't you review for me anyway?"

She nervously swallowed some coffee. "Some of them," she said, "are simply against you and welcome any opportunity to put you down. I think you take a perverse pleasure in offending them. Since you thrive on controversy they're playing right into your schemes."

"We've been through this before, Bunny."

"I know, so I'll go on. Some of the others don't wish to see Jews portrayed as docile."

"What? But that's history!"

"I know that," she said. "And you know that and I'm a little surprised that it's the history teachers who are pushing this kind of opposition."

Bernice looked around, leaned over the table and then fastened her eyes to mine. "Dick Piro, you're not Jewish. I am. And in spite of all this stuff, being Jewish is something wonderful and unique and precious." She was on the edge of tears. I could see her rejecting the line of intelligent logic she had planned. After a hushed, emotional gathering of breath, she said, "How could you, Dick Piro, how could you even think of placing our sacred Jewish traditions, our precious and wonderful and special heritage, into the hands of *those* kids?"

"Bunny," I finally managed, "I really appreciate your confidences but I've got a class and I need a good ten minutes to set up the audio-visual equipment. We're victims of the electronic age and if my filmstrip hookup fails I won't have a thing to say to the class. So, if you'll excuse me, I'll dash. Continue later, OK?"

She tried to smile as she said, "You'll think about what I said?"

"Bernice Rosen, I love you; but that's the first stupid thing you've said today. Will I think about it?"

"OK. OK," she laughed. "Go set up your teaching robot."

I got out of the coffee shop as quickly as possible and then began to shake inside with fury. I was not a "dedicated" teacher. I needed those kids almost to the point of mania. Sometimes I called special rehearsals not because of show requirements but because I was in need of company, not just any company but *their* company, their openness, their innocence in spite of vast experience with what society considered evil. Yes, and their admiration, their need to have someone to whom they could look up who did not look down on them. In spite of being screwed by generations of do-gooders and sadistic authorities, they still managed to come out strong and valuable and overflowing with excellence. They wore their "soul" on the outside. Since the things around me were worn out and unstimulating, I needed their souls. They were fresh. These were *my* kids, dammit.

Bunny certainly knew these things. She knew the depth of my feelings about—not my work—but the children. She obviously did not know me as well as I thought, or else she would not have attempted that particular line of nonreasoning. Whatever she had intended—and she was a shrewd, intelligent woman—it didn't come off. But I had no doubt she had expressed the feelings of the majority of the opposition. It was that basic.

I had come closer to giving up then than I cared to admit. The vastness of the technical jobs awaiting Bruce and me was enough to recommend withdrawal, especially with the limited time remaining before opening night. I could not have weathered another crisis. Perhaps the wisest thing was to go through with *The Crucible.*

All that changed as I went in the main entrance of school. I had been holding two percent of myself in reserve up until my meeting with Bernice. In crossing the street from the restaurant to the school I symbolically crossed the line of commitment. Before then I wouldn't retreat. Now I couldn't. My guts became *Fiddler on the Roof* and I would use every means to see it through to its just Brownsville opening. I could bear personal attack. But when they started on the kids I lost professionalism and vowed total, unlimited war. Thank you, Bunny, I thought. I needed this to really go for score.

It was a Monday in the middle of February, less than three months before opening night. I Scotch-taped a notice on the music-room door announcing the cancellation of Robbins' briefing meeting and got the hell out of there as fast as I could. Bruce and I had work to do.

9

The following morning dawned bright, clear, and eye-watering cold. Involved as I was in *The New York Times* I didn't notice Reginald Barrett, our Perchik, until the subway train lurched as it left the station. He smiled and I indicated the empty seat next to me. He took the sports section while I continued to read the general news. We rode on to Brooklyn in silence. His presence on the train indicated his father had forced the family—mother and four children—to spend the evening with relatives, since he lived a few blocks from school. Some time before, I had asked Reggie about the scar over his right eye. He related that he had received it as a very young child, the result of his father's drinking. At Rockaway Avenue we got off and went down the steps into the blinding sunlight. Reggie had no gloves and his hands quickly turned blue holding his books.

"And how are you this morning, Reb Reggie?" I asked.

"Fine." The flatness of his tone indicated we were not going to play.

"You know, Reg, if I gave you my left glove we both can

have one warm hand in a pocket and one outside holding books."

"No thanks."

"It was a bad night, huh?" I asked gently.

He reached up and rubbed the scar. His voice cracked.

"I hate him," he said.

"Reggie, I—"

"There's nothing you can do, Mr. Piro, so don't ask again."

I took out a handkerchief to wipe my eyes, which were tearing from the sun and the cold.

"Want this?"

"Thanks."

"My eyes are crying from the cold. I don't think yours are, right?"

"Right."

We walked in silence. From across the street James Parker, another member of the cast and Reginald's closest friend, started running in our direction. Reggie quickened his step.

"You don't want to talk to James?"

"Right."

"Sorry, baby, but here he comes."

James fell into step. He was strikingly handsome but so short that he appeared more like a third- or fourth-grader than a junior high school senior about to enter high school. His features were perfectly formed as were the proportions of his body. On the surface he was an exact opposite of Reginald, who was tall, slender, and innocently open in conversation. Just as we greeted each other, we heard a shriek that came from behind us. Rounding the corner were Sheila Haskins and Debra McCall. Both played leads in our show and both were very desirable to the male members of the company. Reginald, like all the boys, had designs on Sheila, but, unlike most of them, was too unsophisticated sexually to understand her game. He thought he had a chance. The girls caught up to us and jostled each other so each could be the first to hug and kiss their "little baby" James. Each girl took one of his hands and we bounced down the street. Reggie fell two steps behind, his big eyes staring straight ahead. In spite of my disapproval of the girls' treatment of James as a mascot, his beaming face was lit with smiles. He seemed perfectly content to hold the hands and occasionally brush his head against their bosoms. Later, each of these gestures would be exaggerated in the telling, which helped to destroy whatever good feelings Reggie was able to muster up concerning his fantasy relationship with Sheila. I had twice warned him that the girls were demeaning James for his size and putting Reggie down by using his best friend as a shield against a more serious association. Reggie preferred to feel rejected and experienced great depths of depression after each encounter with his best friend, James, and his intended girl friend, Sheila. I glanced at Reggie as if to say I understood his daily humiliation. He turned away, took off my glove, and stuffed it into his pocket. Try as I would, I could not get through to this unhappy young man. He suffered alone. I learned to be wary of his feelings during after-school rehearsals. The day's pressures would mount steadily and, after dismissal, the smallest criticism would bring him to tears. Life then seemed so hopeless. His own leading lady, Maritza, to whom he was required to express love on stage, was attractive and seductive. But, as Reggie complained, she was Puerto Rican, which meant she had a very big Puerto Rican boy friend who jealously hovered outside our rehearsals. Reginald was trapped.

The children paused at the main entrance to greet their friends. I moved inside, anxious to get out of the cold. At the top of the steps a voice stopped me.

"Hey, Piro, what's with the meeting yesterday?"

It was the dean of discipline. I didn't like him, nor did I like his tone.

"Wasn't there a notification of cancellation on the door?" I asked.

"Yeah, there was."

"So?"

"I mean, thanks a lot. You schedule something and then you cancel it just like that? I mean how about some warning?"

"Hey, can I talk to you later about this? I want to punch in and get out of these clothes."

I moved down the hall to the general office. Just before entering, Byron Green, a science teacher with whom I had not exchanged two sentences in four years asked, "Why was the *Fiddler* meeting canceled?" I had no idea where he stood on the controversy. His manner indicated annoyance at the lack of a proper cancellation notice.

Throughout the morning I was confronted by teachers expressing similar displeasure. I had been unaware of the amount of concern the *Fiddler* story had generated throughout the staff. To learn that a large percentage of this typically turned-off New York City school faculty had very real feelings concerning the selection of a spring musical was indeed a positive thing. Perhaps I had been wrong in my condemnation of them.

I searched out Abe Gron, union chapter chairman, in the guidance office where he worked as a counselor.

"Abe, a lot of teachers are wild about the meeting. You told me there wasn't any need for it. What's going on?"

"I'm surprised too. I've been getting it all day. I was told that close to thirty teachers showed up and the room was dark."

"I'll take the blame. I forgot to get a notice out so I just posted one on the door before I went home. They did have the right to some prior notice. I know I'd be furious, especially if I had an ax to grind. What should we do?"

"Have a meeting," Abe suggested firmly. "If that's what they want, that's what they'll get."

"Will you take care of it with the boss? I don't think he'll want to see me."

Typical of Abe's efficiency, within the hour a notice was placed in every teacher's mailbox announcing another meeting for the following Wednesday directly after dismissal. This could cause a problem, I thought. Monday was faculty-conference day and the only afternoon most teachers were available after school. On the other days of the week many attended courses or had other responsibilities. I feared we could be accused of scheduling the meeting so that the opposition would be unable to attend without some personal inconvenience. When I communicated all this to Dr. Robbins at lunch he snorted, "Dick Piro, stop looking for ghosts under every bed."

"Dr. Robbins," I said innocently, "do I actually have to tell you not to underestimate Jewish power?"

"Nonsense," he said.

The meeting had been announced for three o'clock, right after pupil dismissal. At two a teacher appeared at the door of my chorus class.

"Dr. Robbins wants to see you immediately. I'll cover the class until you come back."

"Do you know what it's about?"

"No, and I'm damn pissed off that he grabbed me to play nursemaid for the music department. I've got better things to do in my free periods than baby-sit for your chorus."

It was safe to assume a disgruntled parent was in the office demanding to see me. It had happened before. I went down quickly. Dr. Robbins was alone.

"Ten minutes ago," he said, standing behind his chair, "I received a phone call from an organization called Music Theatre International informing me that someone on this staff had reported our forthcoming production of *Fiddler on the Roof* and an immediate law suit is being instituted against us if we persist in going ahead. They're sending it to me in writing tomorrow."

"God bless them," I said, smiling and shaking my head in admiration.

"What's that?" he asked, surprised.

"The opposition. They finally caught on that the easiest way to stop us was to make just this call. It was so simple. My respect for them just went up one hundred points."

"Didn't you tell me you had secured the copyrights?"

"No, Dr. Robbins, I did not tell you that. I told you that through an 'in' I had at the producer's office, there was a sort of tacit agreement not to let one hand know that the other was being washed. I got it in writing. I hoped it would be enough but it won't stand up in court. We've done this before."

"How much are the rights if we got them legally?" he asked.

"You can't get them, which is why so many schools do pirate productions. As long as a show is still in its first run on Broadway, as *Fiddler* is now, no amateur company is legally permitted to touch the show. There's a Broadway company, a national company, and a touring company, period. The rights are *not* available at any cost."

"What about the film proposal? How were you going to hide that?"

"I don't know. Howard Enders has a contract with ABC-TV and we were—"

"ABC?" he shouted. "How the hell did they get in on it?"

"Well, the National Conference of Christians and Jews, who originally wanted the film done, couldn't raise enough funds. National Educational Television refused to see him or his pilot film. So he sold the idea to ABC and will be with them on contract. Don't worry. We'll talk about it. Next week he'll be in to meet you."

Dr. Robbins was not happy with this bit of news. I went on, speaking faster. "Howard and I are both worried about the legalities since media attention requires that we have rights to book, lyrics, and music. The school can do a pirate show but Enders can't make a pirate film."

"Well," Dr. Robbins sighed, "our problems are over now, aren't they? Yours, mine, and Enders'." He searched my face. I realized I was giving him no clue to my feelings about this newest setback. I simply was not feeling. I needed time to digest the defeat. In that instance his news was no worse than an annoying phone call from Teddy informing me he would not be present for a special rehearsal. It was a problem to be solved. I tuned back in to Dr. Robbins.

"We are therefore forced to cancel this production *once and for all.* It would be reprehensible for me to allow it to continue after having been informed through channels about this law. I would be remiss in my responsibilities to the Board of Education in defying the publishers by knowingly going into litigation. I know we don't have a chance."

Through the fog of my own depression I perceived that Robbins was very upset—no—very hurt. I heard him use the word "betrayal." It was my first clear indication that he, too, had had a personal involvement in the show. Again I blanked out. I focused on Robbins' face, thinking, "Well, at least he's off the hook."

I returned to my class just in time for dismissal. Avoiding the appointment I had made with Bruce, I went into the office and called Howard Enders. Flatly I related the situation.

"Are you still having the meeting?" Howard asked.

"I think so. At least he didn't mention that we weren't."

"Can you tape it?"

"What's the point, Howard? It's all over."

"Well, maybe for you but not for me."

"Huh?"

"It's an ending to the film but not the ending I wanted. I mean, Jesus, the story is still there. But I had hoped . . . Who do you think made the call?"

"I don't know, Howard. But I'm sure he won't have the balls to admit it when he sees Robbins' reaction at the meeting."

I left the office and found Bruce in the prop room fixing the wiring on a follow spot. I related what had happened as we walked to the music room.

When I finished, he stood still, staring at the blackboard.

"What about Enders' film?" he asked.

"Oh, I almost forgot. We have to find a way to tape the meeting. Howard needs it as a possible ending."

"OK," Bruce said. "I'll get the machine and put it on the desk."

What are you thinking of? If anyone knew they were being taped there would be hell to pay. We have to do a Bruce Birnel spy thing."

Bruce's face came to life. This was the kind of problem that kept him fascinated with audio equipment year after year. I paced back and forth, trying but still unable to get in touch with the realities of no *Fiddler*. Suddenly Bruce leaped to his feet and said, "Start playing piano and don't stop until I come back."

"Come on, Bruce. I should be insane now, not you."

"Look," he pleaded, "I don't have time. Just do as I say."

"You're nuts."

He threw the *Fiddler* music at me and left. I opened the grand piano and started through the score from the opening theme. After twenty minutes Bruce burst into the room and placed a tape on the playback equipment. I stopped and watched. With a self-congratulatory gesture, Bruce smiled and grandly turned up the volume control. It was my piano playing, unmistakably, errors and all.

"How the hell did you do it?" I asked.

He bobbed his head and grinned. "See that speaker up there?"

"You mean the bitch box for announcements?"

"It's now a microphone," he said, slyly. "I rigged things in the sound-control room so that everything said here is being recorded through it. I'll be here at the start of the meeting and then find an excuse to leave. I'll go downstairs, turn the recorder on, and monitor the levels. Then I'll be back so nobody gets suspicious."

"Bruce, you're brilliant," I saluted. "And to be able to call upon your brilliance in this tragic moment of our defeat when the slings and arrows of defeat are crashing all around us. . . ."

"Fuck you, too."

The bell rang. Classes returned to homerooms for dismissal. I took a folding chair and brought it to the back of the music room. Teachers dribbled in and when I saw them all assembled I was stunned. Close to seventy appeared. It was the largest turnout for a voluntary meeting I had seen in four years at the school, including union meetings. The air was electric. I greeted no one and, blessedly, was not called upon to chat. Closely I watched the entrances of Mitch Grossman, Bunny Rosen, and Aaron Marcus.

A few minutes after three Dr. Robbins came in. The room fell silent. He walked quickly to the center and stood beside the piano. He relaxed, placed his hands at his sides where they remained immobile throughout his talk. He looked especially small.

Dr. Robbins began by giving a low-keyed discourse on the background of the project and his own hesitation over whether he should approve it. Finally he read the letter from the Brownsville Community Council which pledged community support.

"I then discussed the plot of *Fiddler* with several members of the Council," he added. "If you changed the locale and set it in Mississippi, the Russians who performed the pogroms could very well be the Ku Klux Klan of thirty or fourty years ago. The breakup of a family is similar to some of the problems that Puerto Rican people meet when they come to New York, as well as the serf-like condition of the people at that time. Those who had never seen the show did not realize that this was in the play. Even without knowing anything about it, they thought it would be a good idea and my discussion with them made it all the more appropriate. Now, I was amazed to discover that the reason I was doubtful about putting this on—that it might be interpreted as an insult to the community—was not what some members of the teaching staff were concerned about. I found that certain staff members were afraid that Jewish culture and heritage would be placed in a position where it might be ridiculed because of the acting of children or because of the audience. And I was, frankly, amazed, because this had not occurred to me."

As he went on I saw teachers glancing at each other, disturbed. This was not the kind of "meeting" they had anticipated—certainly not a lecture. They had come to debate. Dr. Robbins then chided the group for their unspoken accusation that he and his supervisors would knowingly allow any group's sensitivity to be offended in a public performance.

"I have a feeling," he said, "that were this production done in good taste, with the community's approval, it would probably be the one thing being done in the disadvantaged areas of the city today which would make the papers as something positive.

"Now I must announce to you that somebody—I don't know who it is—made certain telephone calls of complaint yesterday to the district superintendent's office. This, in itself, wasn't too bad. I can deal with the superintendent's anger. But shortly before two P.M. I received a telephone call from Music Theatre International—the organization that controls the copyrights to *Fiddler*—informing me that they have not authorized the release of *Fiddler on the Roof* and they will institute legal action against us if we put on the show. The gentleman said that they will make no concessions whatever. They're a business organization and couldn't care less that we have certain relationships which we are trying to build up here. So we cannot put this production on here."

There was a sudden intake of breath. Fidgeting ceased. Robbins, normally so fluent in speech, began groping for words. At times he lost his train of thought. I had never seen him behave this way. None of us had.

"Now let me tell you what this means to you and me. I'm going to write to the Brownsville Community Council and tell them that we can't put on this production because we haven't got the legal rights. And they'll ask us why we didn't know this in advance. And if we knew we couldn't get legal rights, why did we start the whole business in the first place? How come Music Theatre International found out all of a sudden? Because of antipathy, somebody—staff or community or child—has structured a far worse barrier between this school and this community than would have existed had we done the show. The person or persons who made this call, I think, has struck the worst blow at this school since I've been here. We can live with our daily problems, that's what we get paid for. We can endure new teachers and hope they work out. We can do the best we can with children. But there's one thing we can't do and that is survive in a community that hates us. And this community does not hate us. It dislikes what some of us have done, just as I dislike some of the things they have done. But it doesn't hate us. The community has, up to now, been willing to play ball. But I can't say what will happen now. But this—and I'm talking about insults—is the most grievous and most flagrant kind of insult that can be conceived of by me."

He paused. His eyes roamed over the room and finally rested on me. Totally without emotion he said, "So the show won't be put on; as far as I'm concerned, it can't be put on. I will keep you informed about what the result will be when I write the letter tomorrow or the day after to the Brownsville Community Council. I'm going to tell them exactly what happened. They will think that we have been stringing them along for all this time. And there's no way of tackling this except to be forthright. A discussion as to whether we should or should not have put on *Fiddler on the Roof* is now irrelevant."

Dr. Robbins was finished. He had given no indication that the teachers should disperse, and no one knew what to do. Bruce broke the silence: "Dr. Robbins, I wouldn't give up the ship entirely. I've been in the music-making business for a long time and I'm certain I know some people that may be able to run interference for us with the publishers. At least I'll try."

The staff turned anxiously to look at Bruce. I felt the majority abhorred the method used to stop this show. At one point they might have rejoiced that it was finished. Now they weren't sure.

Dr. Robbins turned to leave the room. The group quickly followed.

"Do you really know anyone?" I asked Bruce.

"No," he replied. "I just wanted to shake up those bastards."

"Who do you think it was?"

"Have you any doubt? Hey, wait a minute. How sure are we that someone didn't call and claim he was from Music Theatre International? Maybe the call was a fake. Anyone could look at the sheet music and tell who the publisher was."

"Good show, Bruce. Let's check it out. Meet me downstairs in the office."

Within minutes I learned that the call to the publishers had been placed by Aaron Marcus. While he denied the act to several people, he couldn't help bragging about his coup to his friends, who immediately exonerated their own guilt by informing me. The story went that he had described the controversy to a lawyer friend while at a party. The lawyer suggested he inform the publishers. He started by calling G. Schirmer, a music dealer, and worked up to the publisher.

School emptied of students and teachers. As Bruce and Amelia Brown—who was in a worse state of shock than I—stood by, I dialed Music Theatre International and asked to speak to the person who had had a conversation that afternoon with a junior-high-school principal in Brooklyn. The lawyer was found.

"Hi," I said. "My name is Dick Piro. I understand you had a conversation with my principal this afternoon about our production of *Fiddler on the Roof*?"

"Say, what's going on down there?" he asked. "I was just doing my job to protect our writers and your boss hung up on me. I explained the situation and he said, 'Put it in writing and send it to me,' and then slammed down the phone."

"Because," I said quickly, "he was betrayed and because he is a fantastic educator and because he was smart enough to project an entire new crisis the instant he realized who and what you represented."

"I don't understand."

I related the story. At the end, the lawyer took a deep breath and said, "Mr. Piro, as a Jewish boy from Brooklyn, raised not too far from your school, I must say that I am embarrassed down to my toes. Listen. Let me make some phone calls and I'll get back to you tomorrow. I'm not promising you anything but hang on a day, will you? I've already sent out the letter to your boss but don't pay it much attention, OK?"

It wasn't much. But for Bruce, Amelia, and myself, it was a blinding ray of sunshine. We hugged each other and cursed all of the minutes we were forced to wait until the next day.

My first act that evening was to call Frances Brown and Lil Carter to tell them exactly what had happened including Aaron Marcus' alleged role in it. I realized to what degree Robbins had played the devil's advocate and I set about presenting Robbins as a fallen hero. Thus Mrs. Brown and Mrs. Carter held no suspicions of an administrative swindle.

The next afternoon the lawyer called to give me the name and number of Harold Prince's lawyer at the William Morris Agency. Mr. Prince was the producer of the original *Fiddler.* I contacted the agency immediately. Once facts were verified, they were anxious to rescue what seemed like a doomed situation. A day later it was officially suggested that we go on with the project. Ambiguous as to exact details, it was nearly guaranteed we would receive the necessary permission.

Triumphantly I reported those three days' events to Dr. Robbins. It was the first time we had spoken since the meeting. I preferred to wait for positive news.

"I'll believe it when I see it in writing," he scoffed. "Therefore, until I do—and I doubt if big business cares a fig about our problems—the production is still officially canceled. What you do about rehearsals is your own business."

His careful reading of the word "officially" was a green light to go on working. But his insistence on permission in writing created a new problem. The publishers suggested we go ahead and I was grateful. This was enough. But urging them to put it in writing immediately might turn them off. We were walking a thin line.

Several phone calls later I learned that Joe Stein, author of *Fiddler*, Sheldon Harnick (lyrics) and Jerry Bock (music) —who together owned sixty percent of their show—had indicated to their agents, lawyers, and publishers that we were to be given permission in writing provided we printed a blurb on our program stating that a "special arrangement" had been made with Music Theatre International. Their permission arrived in writing within a week.

Later that day I was called to the phone. A secretary shrieked, "It's Joe Stein, the *writer* of *Fiddler on the Roof*!" A crowd gathered in the office to monitor this call from a real celebrity. Mr. Stein said he was pleased to have us do his show and agreed that it might have an impact on human relations. He pledged full support and urged that we call upon him or anyone from the Broadway staff for help in solving any problems, whether they were technical, script, or lighting. He ended by asking me to call periodically at his private number to keep him abreast of the progress of the production, finally thwarting all my efforts to express gratitude. I learned later that he was the one responsible for setting all the machinery in motion resulting in our receiving permission.

The children did not overreact with cheering as they had the last time. They had long lost sight of the real issues and the situation deteriorated down to Mr. Piro against all of *them*. Whatever teacher offended any one of the children, including those who were making normal demands for academic achievement, became a "them."

One afternoon, to my horror, I saw Nat Goldberg, English teacher, being pursued by a group of sixth-graders all shouting, "Hello, Goldie!" His white hair flew as he turned abruptly in the hallway and tried to catch the nearest taunting child. They all screamed with glee and fled up the stairs to the next landing where they continued to ridicule him until he passed out of sight. I waited until he was alone and approached him. I was furious with the children for doing this to him.

"Mr. Goldberg," I said, apologetically. "I'm terribly sorry. I swear to God it will never happen again."

"Hell," he replied. "I love it. It's just a game we're playing."

"You mean, it's just a game?"

"Sure. It started a few days ago. They really enjoy it. So do I. Makes walking these dreary halls easier to take. It's a line from *Fiddler,* you know. Yente's opening words to Golde."

"Thank you, Mr. Goldberg. I needed something like this."

"My name's Nat, you know."

"Thanks, Nat. I'll see you around."

The children slew the windmill and we were whizzing towards opening night, two months and God knew how many cancellations away.

10

TO: Drama Class
FROM: R. J. Piro
SUBJECT: Fiddler on the Roof Progress Report #1

Overheard in the prop room last year: "Progress Reports? Oh, that's when Mr. Piro gets in a funk about the show."

May the person who said that itch in places he can't reach--it's that close to the truth. The person went on to say, "When Mr. Piro feels good about the show he writes to us how terrible we are and when he feels bad he writes how good we all are." Right now, gang, I feel terrible fear for all of us.

I've looked and looked at this script and its full of problems for Mr. Birnel and me, but not too many for you that a few hours of line studying couldn't solve. It's a GOOD show and, for some reason it really got to me today and I found myself crying in many spots. (I snuck up to Broadway and saw it again for the umpteenth time today.) During the ups and downs of our struggle to put it on I admit that I wavered, but now I am strong and firm in the belief that it is the right show for us at the right time. So what's bothering me? I really don't know. I do know that at this point in a show preparation I am usually scared to death because, in addition to worrying about you and your lines, and your moves, and your loud-and-clear projection, I also have scenery, costumes, makeup, lights, dancing, programs, tickets, publicity, etc., etc., etc., to put me in an insane institution (in addition to the one I now attend in Brooklyn).

The degree of tension right now determines the degree of pure ecstasy when this thing finally gets put on the boards. Hey, it'll be brilliant!!!

I've got to sleep. Do you think if I knocked out one of my teeth and put it under my pillow the good fairy would leave me a sound track of the show instead of a quarter? No, it's not worth a try, Duane! God, I'm scared. But why do I feel so good?

The excitement of the past weeks leveled off and we found ourselves in "normal" play preparation. Active opposition ceased. Dr. Robbins suspected that opposing teachers finally realized their victimization by overzealous leaders. Bruce and I luxuriated in the exclusive concentration on production tasks.

Midweek I found a message in my mail box with instructions to call a Mr. Green at CBS. Several attempts to reach him proved fruitless, and my curiosity about who and what he was increased. As a last ditch effort, I called from a phone booth in the Times Square subway station. Over the roar of trains I learned he was a director of radio news. He asked if I were willing to appear on a morning radio talk show, sponsored by the news department. My first question was, "How did you hear about us and how much do you know of what's going on?" His response seemed deliberately ambiguous.

"I would love to do it," I told him. "But since it involves school time I will have to get permission from my principal. Why don't you call Dr. Robbins tomorrow morning and, assuming he agrees, I'll get back to you in the afternoon. My rehearsal ends at 4:30."

"Fine," he said. "Talk to you tomorrow."

The next day I received a terse summons from Dr. Robbins. I went into his office just before lunch. He jumped up and closed the door. Trembling with fury, he mumbled over and over again, "How dare they. How *dare* they!"

Few, if any, knew Dr. Robbins' thoughts during the teacher strike. We knew he remained out of work and took this as overt support. But then I realized the degree of this support. Along with most administrators, he held the media in contempt for their one-sided reporting during the crisis. Piecing together both sides of the story, I later learned that when CBS called, Dr. Robbins lost his temper and, taking hold of the opportunity to strike back, raved for thirty minutes about misuse of public responsibility. He had hoped that we were through with the *Fiddler* controversy. Radio Station WCBS represented a fresh opening of the wound and would bring all sorts of "nut groups" down upon our school to further agitate. He most certainly would not approve Mr. Piro's appearance on a radio show. WCBS was to get the hell away and leave us alone. Robbins had a good point but, as a showman, I was personally disappointed. I would have enjoyed the appearance and we all could have used the publicity.

As an aftermath of the strike some black hate-groups had pledged to destroy the "white pigs" who were holding children in the slavery of ignorance. They began as a nuisance but, playing on fear, were steadily gaining power in the ghettos. Threats of violence were not limited to whites but to anyone who stood in their way. If it were known publicly that a group of Jews were in opposition to black aspirations, our building would then be prey to a holocaust in which none of us would be safe. Dr. Robbins was scared and, after our talk, I was scared, too. Good-bye WCBS.

That afternoon between the end of music classes and the start of after-school rehearsal, Dr. Robbins entered the auditorium by a side entrance. I was surprised. He did not generally come backstage. While accepting the fact that a certain amount of theatrical litter was unavoidable, he chose not to see it. He realized it was impossible to produce high-caliber shows without breaking some fire regulations. He was thus covering himself by avoiding the prop-room area.

"Hi, Dr. Robbins. The kids will be right in. What can I do for you?"

Too casually, I dropped my cigarette and ground it out. He saw it and frowned.

"Tomorrow afternoon between two and three, CBS-TV will be here with their roving reporter, Jean Parr. They intend to film for a TV news broadcast. God help us all afterwards."

"What? But we were involved with radio. Remember radio?"

"It seems," he said, "that I offended the radio director, so he got on the phone with the big TV guys. They then called the district superintendent and threatened to break the story wide open. Evidently they called the Board of Education, too. The district superintendent was caught in a squeeze and gave them permission, in spite of my objections."

"Boy, when they want something they sure—"

"It's up to you, Dick."

"What do you mean, 'up to me'?"

"You must do everything in your power to see that this film is limited to your work and the kids' work. If news of the Jewish business gets out we are dead in this school. You may not be able to hold them back but at least try. For God's sake try."

He left as the children entered. They caught my mood and did not perform the usual prerehearsal nonsense such as ball playing in the pit, playing tag along the rows of seats, and turning up their transistor phonographs all at the same time.

"Please sit down immediately," I directed. "I've got something important to announce."

The early arrivals took seats down front to the surprise of the others who hit the door with the usual raucous noise. We waited for Teddy. Arriving late was part of his "star" training, according to the rest of the cast. He finally showed up, saw us sitting quietly and said, "Oh shit! Canceled again?"

The children laughed.

I asked, "How many of you think that's what I've got to announce?"

All raised their hands except Beverly.

"Beverly, why don't you think so?"

"Because, Mr. Piro, you have a very evil grin hiding just behind your eyes. If 'they' got to us again, you'd be pacing back and forth instead of sitting on top of the piano. You only sit there when you're happy."

"Beverly," I asked, "what are you planning on becoming, in addition to a fantastic actress?"

"A psychiatrist."

"Don't bother. Just put your shingle out."

The children sharpened their interest. Duane stood up.

"Then you mean our show's not canceled again?"

"No, Duane."

"Yippee!" His outburst was taken up by the others.

When they became quiet again, I asked, "Does anyone here know the name Jean Parr?"

"You mean the Channel Two lady on the six-o'clock news?" Duane asked.

"Right, Duane. I never watch TV so I wasn't sure of the name."

"She's bad," Tina interjected.

"What's wrong with her?" I challenged.

"Come on, Mr. Piro," Tina responded. "You've been with us long enough to know what 'bad' means. It means great."

"Anyway," I continued, "she's coming here tomorrow with a film crew to do a news segment."

The children exploded. I waited. When they were calm again I said, "They'll be here between two and three, which means Dr. Robbins has given you all permission to come down last period instead of going to class. Therefore, I want everyone to go directly to the prop room and get in costume. Only light makeup, except for Teddy. We'll do 'Tradition' and maybe 'Matchmaker' since the house interior is almost finished. I want to show off a little bit of our set."

"Are you going to write us out a pass?" asked Lolita.

"No. There isn't time. After class why don't you all hunt up your eighth-period teachers and inform them in person? Don't be fresh about it. Tell them that you have to be here for a TV tape session. They won't believe you but try it anyway."

CBS-TV arrived on schedule the next afternoon with a mountain of equipment. The children made up quickly and ran into the auditorium to watch the crews unload. The back of the auditorium was crowded with teachers who had come to catch a glimpse of Jean Parr. The cast assembled in the pit to hear notes prior to a "normal" rehearsal. We went through some music while the TV crew took readings and checked light levels on stage. In the middle of the organized confusion Linus Sellars, our Russian lover, sauntered out of the prop room twenty minutes late. I stopped the music and looked at him.

"Linus, your new white sneakers are lovely."

"Thanks," he said, waiting for my followup remark.

"Since I don't think rubber was yet invented in 1902 I would prefer that you wear shoes. It really annoys me to have to even suggest this. You're playing a lead in this show. Do I have to dress you too?"

"I forgot them."

"You what?"

"I forgot to bring shoes. We had gym fourth period and I usually just wear sneakers all day."

"How often do you have gym?"

"Twice a week."

"For how long?"

"Three years now. Why?"

"How often have you appeared on television?"

"This is my first time."

"Did you know about this TV session?"

"Of course. I was here yesterday when you announced it."

"OK, Linus. We'll have to tape without you."

"Fine," he said, anxious to project a consistently calm attitude. He remained standing.

"You can go, Linus. We won't be needing you today."

He paused and stared directly into my eyes. I would have welcomed a loss of temper since his attempts to appear cool were a source of irritation for all of us. His eyes filmed with an unspoken promise to revenge the moment. He turned and left the room. The children looked at me with reproach. I had prevented Linus from getting on television just because he wore a pair of sneakers. Cast members sneaked back into the prop room to retrieve lost yarmulkes and other smaller pieces of costuming. A point was made. Linus had served the company well.

Just then Jean Parr stormed down to the pit followed by a camera and script man.

"What kind of chicken teachers do you have in this school?" she demanded. The children snickered. "Not one of those creeps back there is willing to make an on-camera statement. Now, I *know* things have not been a bed of roses around here."

"Miss Parr, the teachers in this building are—"

"Look, Mr. Piro," she interrupted, "I haven't any time for games. I'm here for *news*. The Jewish resistance to this play is news."

In the middle of my attempt at Robbins-type diplomacy she rushed back up the aisle and threatened the teachers with an exposé if they continued in their refusal to make statements.

It was time to shoot. She began with six teachers including Bunny Rosen and Shelly Katz. They were dressed in overcoats preparatory to leaving for home in the cold winter weather. The faces of the men showed their five-o'clock shadows. They were bunched together as if they felt intimidated. Miss Parr shot questions at them. They barely responded. She asked, "What is your opinion of the director of *Fiddler*?" There was a pause finally broken by Shelly, the teacher who had refused to take "scabs" home in his car. He stepped forward and said, "No comment." Their statements boiled down to the fact that each felt we should have explored theater involving Afro-American or Afro-Caribbean cultural aspirations. With poor lighting, natural fear of publicity, and restrained animosity towards this threatening woman, the teachers came across badly. It was unfair to them.

Dr. Robbins was next. Together we had been watching the previous segment from the pit. The children were sitting quietly, tense with excitement at witnessing a "real live filmed news broadcast." Reluctantly Dr. Robbins moved to the stage, passing the interviewed teachers and nodding in sympathy. Towering above him, Jean Parr asked for his views. He gave a tight, articulate presentation, admitting that he had misjudged the feelings of the community but that now he was pleased to see the school functioning closely with parents. During his statement Duane whispered to me, "I don't understand what he's saying, do you?"

"He's admitting to eight million New Yorkers that he was wrong," I said.

"Wow!"

"You won't find many principals like this one, Duane, if you go to school for the rest of your life."

I was next. The children urged me on to the stage with, "Go git 'em, Mr. Piro." Jean Parr shook my hand. The kids applauded. Silence returned. She looked directly at me and asked, "Exactly what were your reasons for selecting *Fiddler on the Roof*?" I turned away for a second, framing my reply. When I looked at her she had moved away to confer with a technician. Since the cameras were still going I assumed she expected me to continue. It happened again and I thought, "How the hell can you get anything going if the woman turns away after every question? She obviously doesn't give a damn about the answer." Eventually I looked at a chair in the second row while concentrating on my responses.

She then asked us to rehearse a musical number. I called for the girls in "Matchmaker" and the piece was filmed, including Teddy's monologue. The show pieces over, she moved in on the cast for single interviews. We held our breath. I whispered to Dr. Robbins, "See, she's playing it cool. Everything's going to be all right."

"We won't know that until we see it," he snorted. "With over-dubbing she has the power to portray any attitude she wants." She gathered up Teddy, Beverly, Reggie, and some others. All spoke about people getting together through the script. These were familiar questions and the children responded with their customary answers. Teddy, ever the performer, was not content with routine interviews. He used his character of Tevye and with characteristic gestures consistently interjected, "As the good book says." Jean Parr asked him, "Who, exactly, was Tevye?" Teddy looked away, grinned into the camera, comfortable and secure, and answered simply, "Tevye was a poor milkman who lived in a ghetto, just like we do."

The last student interviewed was Rita Small. She was a big girl and then president of the student-government organization. With a voice like Mahalia Jackson, she was playing the role of Grandma Tzeitel in the "Dream Sequence." Amelia Brown, recognizing Rita's considerable leadership powers, had sponsored her campaign for the presidency. This was Rita's first real chance to exercise power. She looked through the group of technicians and found my face and grinned conspiratorially. Then, to our horror, she blew the story wide open by viciously attacking the Jewish teachers by name.

"I mean," she said, "Just because Mr. Piro digs kids they are trying to get him and they give us bad marks because we're in *Fiddler*. They're very unfair because they're lousy teachers, anyway."

She warmed to the subject and was pleased with what she had said, thinking she was helping us and certain of gaining our approval. Dr. Robbins groaned. Teachers, frightened, hastened to leave. Jean Parr and CBS finally had what they wanted. News of the Jewish resistance to our show was out. We cleared the room.

That evening CBS aired the story on the news at both six and eleven o'clock. To my relief Jean Parr had edited Rita's exposition leaving just her positive statements on film. Only those who had been near enough to hear the full conversation could possibly have known that an editing job had been done. It was amazing and frightening to see what the media could do to a conversation, albeit in our favor. Rita came through as a bright teen-ager in spite of the fact that what the viewer heard was a compilation of several unrelated statements. The teacher interviews came through badly, and I expected adverse reactions.

Just after the six-o'clock telecast I called Robbins.

"Hi, Dr. Robbins."

"Dick, I've got to say it. Every time you fall into a sewer you come up holding a gold watch."

"Thanks. What about yourself? What did you think?"

"I looked old and tired."

"Nonsense. You looked terrific."

"Come on, Dick."

"What about your responses to the questions? You've got to admit that you came off well there."

"Well," he said, grudgingly, "I was surprised I said all that I did."

"Surprised?"

"Dick, the only thing I was really thinking of was why the hell must this giant of a woman stand so close? I had to tilt my chin up to see her face."

All was well. If he could banter he was pleased. We had had a close brush with disaster.

The next day we were inundated with phone calls from outside of our school district requesting tickets. Several asked for rights to photo studies. We granted *New York* magazine permission to do a story provided it stressed the work of the kids. *Woman's Day* made an appointment for interviews, and both French National Television and the Canadian Broadcasting Corporation requested filming dates. Radio station WBAI (which had stirred trouble by broadcasting the anti-Semitic poem) set legal action in motion giving them permission to air a tape of the opening night. The children kept accounts of the various requests and sought me out between classes for the latest "points." Characteristically, most of them were surprised that so many people were interested in their activities.

It was one of Teddy's "sleep-in" days and he arrived at school late. I rescued him from the hands of the disciplinarians and walked him in the direction of his class.

"Well, star, how did your mother like it?"

"She finally managed to believe me."

"What do you mean 'believe you'?" I asked.

"I told her we would be on, right? And then she doesn't believe me. So she starts getting ready to go out about five-thirty. She's in the bedroom and I drag in the TV and plug it in. Then she goes to the bathroom and I plug it in there. All the time she's calling me a liar. Finally at six when we came on I caught her just going out the door. So she sat and watched. I was so tired I just lay on the floor and watched it upside down."

"Boy, you sure were relaxed—on camera I mean—not watching it. How come?"

"Who, me? I seen this woman so much she's like a relative. I just pretended I was in my own house watching her ask me questions from behind the screen. Then I just jived. She's my friend almost." We parted at the music room as he strutted down the corridor, basking in his notoriety.

At three o'clock I received a message which turned out to be an invitation to appear on the Barry Farber Show, an all-night radio talk program. For most of my adult life I had been listening to these shows with curiosity. Now I would find out. I took the request to Robbins as a courtesy. Since it was to take place from 11:15 P.M. to 4 A.M. he had no power to stop it, as he had with WCBS. His first reaction was a question.

"Who else is going to be on the show?"

"I don't really know," I said truthfully. "Some rabbi who runs a group called the Jewish Defense League, and some B'nai Brith—"

"No. No. No!" he cried.

"Why?"

"Do you know what the Jewish Defense League is?"

"Is that the group that puts vigilantes in Jewish neighborhoods to retaliate against black violence?"

"Right. Their leader, Rabbi Meir Kahane, will cut you to shreds. I've heard this guy in action. Dick, he'll slaughter you. It is my strongest wish that you turn down this invitation."

"Dr. Robbins," I pleaded, "everything that has come out of *Fiddler* up to now has been for the kids, the show, and the community. I want to do this radio show."

"What do you hope to gain?"

"Personal experience. Trivia."

We parted at an impasse. Later that day he sent a formal letter requesting I reconsider my decision. I ignored it.

The Barry Farber Show was a total bore. The rabbi felt that our *Fiddler on the Roof* plans represented the most positive and encouraging thing to happen between Jews and blacks in at least a generation. No argument; consequently, no meaningful discussion. The bulk of the show was taken up with a confrontation between the militant Jewish Defense League and the B'nai Brith, with two militant black ladies in between.

The afternoon following the CBS-TV interviews was particularly busy with several General Music periods scheduled. These classes represented the music staff's most trying times. Each group contained a minimum of sixty boys and girls who met only once a week. As a result it was almost impossible to build personal relationships between the teacher and students. Proper attendance procedures were useless and sessions were interrupted with intruders claiming it was their class, and, of course, many students cut each week. We had a minimum of two instructors assigned, one as teacher, the other as assistant. Because of attendance problems there was a serious lack of teaching continuity. Each teacher found his own solutions (some found none and simply played rock 'n' roll records each week). Mine was in the nature of a nightclub act revolving around analysis of classical music pieces.

On that particular afternoon I arrived in class followed by

Beverly, Mary, and Duane. They were too excited about the previous evening's TV broadcast to attend their own classes and were remaining with me for the day. Entering the music room we encountered an argument among several boys. Some insisted the TV program didn't take place, while the others said it had.

It took five minutes to bring the class to attention. I asked, "How many of you saw us on TV last night?" About half the class had. The others looked angry.

"I saw that corny show," scoffed a boy in the back.

The music-analysis lesson plan was thrown out and we spent the period talking about the techniques involved in making a ten-minute news segment. Most students were in conflict because their images of themselves had suddenly changed. The majority of the students in Junior High School 275 believed they were second-class citizens. They had to be. Being black and poor and living in a slum did not entitle them to any kind of positive national attention. Television was the *Alice in Wonderland* mirror. Race riots in Detroit and Newark and the Lawrence Welk show were all fantasy to them. Yet they had seen Teddy, Beverly, Duane, Mary, their principal, and me on the news. It was upsetting and didn't click with being forgotten and defeated. I spent the week attempting to affirm the realities of our worth to the nation. They refused to believe. I was reminded of Dr. Robbins' challenge when he interviewed me for the job four years before. He felt this was the major obstacle working against the ghetto teen-ager. He had said, "Until these boys and girls realize their unlimited potential as first-class citizens, they'll never get out of the ghetto. I believe most strongly in the performing arts because here excellence is a reality. With the taste of success in their mouths perhaps they will go for similar sensations in the academic areas of reading, math, and science."

February 3, 1969

TO: Cast & Crew of Fiddler of TELEVISION Fame.

FROM: R. J. Piro (The Sicilian Catholic?)

SUBJECT: Progress Report #3

By now you must all be pretty proud of yourselves. Well, if you're not, I am. I was so pleased with your professionalism during the TV taping. You were quiet, extremely cooperative, interested, interesting, and very mature in your response to the whole thing. All these things were much more important to me than the actual performance you were supposed to do. You came through with flying colors. (No pun intended, Duane.)

Hey, how about that! Two TV showings in one evening. (No, I didn't know it was going to be on the 11 o'clock news so I didn't see it that time.) Now where do we go from here? What a responsibility we all have! The whole city and probably the nation know about this project and our job now is to DELIVER the best damn show ever performed anywhere. There isn't a question about it. WE MUST DO IT!!! Last year we had a great show and begged (in writing) the power structure--mayor, superintendent, Brownsville Community Council, local politicians--to attend and they didn't show. This year they are falling all over us looking for tickets! Is it going to be worth it?

We were ready to thank our community for their support and present an hour's segment of *Fiddler* for the monthly PTA meeting, complete with costumes, lighting, and makeup. I was nervous. If the show didn't click, cast morale would plummet. If the audience did not respond to the humor and the pathos of the story, we had spent four agonizing months in vain. It was to be a preview performance without the option of rewrites if the script didn't work. This was it, folks. Take it or leave it.

Since average PTA attendance seldom exceeded thirty out of a possible seventeen hundred parents, we decided to increase attendance by having the two-hundred-voice chorus perform a section of their *Testament of Freedom* cantata. Parents generally turned out to see their own children perform and we expected at least two hundred and fifty guests.

Wednesday night arrived, two weeks after the CBS show. With over five hundred parents in the auditorium, the room was uncomfortably hot and humid. I insisted, over custodial objections, that the blower system be turned off because the humming noise of the fans made it difficult for the actors and singers to project.

The chorus performed first and did themselves proud. Thomas Jefferson's texts justifying violence against British oppression never seemed more relevant. When they were finished, the stage was cleared for the opening number of *Fiddler*. From my place in the pit I noticed some children leaning over a spot downstage left. It was a pool of vomit. During the *Testament of Freedom* a child had been sick. I was extremely proud that the chorus had ignored this distraction to give a superb performance. We sent for mops and a cleanup crew. Bruce was in the wings organizing his lighting crew while I adjusted the taped accompaniment in the pit. The audience relaxed between performances with the house lights on half level.

I saw a black man between forty and fifty years old leave his seat and approach the then open, blank stage. He was dressed in old, dirty clothes, sneakers with holes at the toes, a shirt with one sleeve torn off, and trousers held up with a piece of rope. He walked down the aisle, climbed the three stairs on the right and moved drunkenly to stage center. Audience chatter fluttered to a stop. Cast faces appeared in the wings looking to me for an explanation. The man turned to the audience, leered, and began making obscene gestures. Bruce approached from the side. The intruder resisted his gentle request to leave and shoved him back with a force that belied his drunken or drugged state. The audience gasped. Bruce's first reaction was to shout to the boys on the opposite side, "Close the outside curtains."

I jumped to the microphone and attempted a bluff as the curtains closed.

"Would any one of you teachers standing in the back please summon the policeman on duty in the hall?"

A parent rose from his seat and came quickly towards me. It was Mr. Haskins, whose daughter, Sheila, was playing the part of Chava in the evening's performance.

"Mr. Piro, do you need any help?" he asked nervously.

"I sure do."

He leaped onto the stage and went through the center cut of the outside curtains. I heard children screaming and some heavy scuffling. Mr. Haskins asked the man to come along and received an angry shove. Haskins then grabbed the man in a hammerlock, picked him up, and carried him outside into the corridor. As I ran out the side exit near the prop room I heard the intruder scream, "Help, *brothers,* help!" My heart froze as I looked up and down the empty corridor. This was the black call to arms. Granted, a black man was being held at bay by another black, but by the time the cause of the incident was revealed, many people could be seriously hurt. This was riot material. Luckily, there were no "brothers" within hearing and a police officer showed up to take over.

I returned inside the auditorium and introduced the first act of *Fiddler on the Roof*. But my mind was not on the performance. I was concentrating on the fact that out of five hundred adults, one parent thought enough of the safety of the children to offer his assistance. In front of five hundred people, and in a public school auditorium, we still could not guarantee rational behavior. Anyone could walk up those three stairs and take over this assembly. These people were as terrified of violence as I was. I remembered my mugging. With a superhuman effort, I wrenched my thoughts from hopelessness and focused on the stage and the children. They would demand specific comments from me later about each bit of stage business. I had to be ready.

The performance was a revelation. We knew there was humor in *Fiddler on the Roof* but not one of us, child or adult, had had the slightest idea how it would strike a predominantly black audience. Hardly a cast member did not have a parent or relative in domestic service for a white family. In many instances they worked for white Jewish families. It was showdown night.

After the opening, "Tradition"—which received good, solid applause—the play began. The audience is brought into a frenzied household with Golde, the classic Jewish mother, and her five daughters preparing the Sabbath dinner, fussing that her husband, Tevye, as usual, will be late. Into the chaos comes Yente, the matchmaker, on a business-social call. Golde hustles the children out and settles down to find out what Yente has done for her oldest daughter, Tzeitel. Rather than sit in the chair offered to her, Yente subtly removes a cloth from her enormous carpetbag and lightly dusts the seat. Golde notes this slur on her housekeeping abilities and is furious. But she holds her reactions inside. She needs Yente. When Golde is not looking, Yente rearranges the placement of silverware on the Sabbath table. Golde, in turn, replaces the silver to its original position. All this is accomplished over a running dialogue concerning the problems of raising children and finding suitable husbands for a family "blessed" with five daughters.

Forget Jewish. Forget black. Forget Puerto Rican. The audience was completely captivated by two women doing the universal thing. The girls onstage—Olga as Yente and Beverly as Golde—rode the laughter with newer and funnier business. They took their time and were not anxious to fill each second on stage with dialogue. This is the essence of real acting. I expected them to be thrown by the audience laughter. They weren't; they increased the reality with pregnant pauses.

Women in the audience were back-slapping each other and vocally responding to the action with, "Go git her, sister," and "Give her body, honey," and, of course, "All *right*!" Olga received thunderous applause upon her exit.

The director in me was alarmed. Olga was, by academic standards, the brightest child in the show. She had no trouble memorizing geometry theorems but she could not memorize a line and keep it intact. Her mind leapt to limitless possibilities and in each speech she departed from the original, until by opening night I expected a rewritten role. In rehearsals Olga would begin, "Golde, my darling, I just had to see you because I have such wonderful news for you."

"Olga, stop," I ordered. "Open your script. Now read."

"Golde darling, I had to see you because I have such news for you," she read dutifully.

"So?" I asked.

"So?" she mimicked. "What's the difference? You said we should make it real."

"Olga, I love you, but I'm going to kill you anyway. The strength in *Fiddler* rests with certain Jewishness in characters such as Yente."

"So why won't you let me use an accent and my hands the way I used to?"

"Because," I patiently explained for the hundredth time, "it is false, pretentious, and offensive. Jewishness then as well as now rests with a certain speech rhythm."

"So?" she persisted. "Why can't I change that rhythm and use my own?"

"That's a very good question, Olga. I would say you

couldn't because these rhythms took hundreds of years to evolve. I, not being Jewish, cannot evaluate what you make up. So we have a script, right?"

"Right."

"So why should both of us sweat when with just a few extra moments you can memorize exactly what is on the page, right?"

"Wrong."

My patience was about to run out.

"Olga," I said through clenched teeth. "Are you trying to tell me that you are too intelligent to memorize something exactly as written? Be careful of your answer, because people that bright we don't need. If everyone else can do it you can. If not, I'll be glad to relieve you of acting responsibilities. I'm a little tired of cheating the other kids out of my time because I have to baby-sit with your brain."

By opening night few of her lines conformed to the script. She "worked" at the character and, though audiences found her delightful, that five percent between excellence and perfection was missing. Luckily Yente exits after her one big opening scene and then becomes part of the ensemble almost until the end of Act II when she has another solo bit. We added much physical material and this, coupled with Beverly's perfect Golde, basic humor, and good writing, carried the scenes. Olga never had the opportunity of relaxing within a framework of set lines. Each rehearsal and performance became a new and agonizing experience in improvisation.

Later I learned that Olga's serious stage fright carried into rehearsals. She, bless her, did not communicate her fears to me and it wasn't until I was sitting at her mother's dinner table on closing night that I realized the extent of her agony. She had protected me from a problem. Had she been less bright and more selfish, I could have helped her out of her fears and mine.

A highlight of that PTA evening performance was Duane's breakthrough in the character of Motel, the shy tailor. Early in Act I we learn that Tzeitel, Tevye's eldest daughter, is in love with her playmate from childhood. They hope to be married. Since he is so terribly poor the parents never consider him a suitable match. Tzeitel begs him to speak to her father, but he can't because of shyness—in Tevye's ominous presence he stammers only common pleasantries. Tzeitel meets him in the kitchen while setting the Sabbath table and informs him that Yente, the matchmaker, has already made a business call, probably with news about finding her a husband in the village. She fears their dreams of a life together are dashed unless he speaks to her father immediately—that night before dinner. He promises to do so.

When Tevye comes home there is pandemonium in the house, with greetings of "Good Sabbath," and curiosity about the guest, Perchik, that Tevye has brought home. Tevye sets about washing his hands and donning special Sabbath garments. Motel follows him stuttering, "R-R-Reb Tevye."

"Well, what is it, Motel? I'm busy."

Tevye continues preparations as Motel dogs his every step. Tevye becomes more and more annoyed. Finally they collide head on. Motel cowers as Tevye looks down and shouts in a booming voice, "Well, what is it, Motel?"

Motel stands frozen. He cannot swallow. He cannot breathe. He cannot move from his spot of terror, while Tevye stands tapping his foot with impatience. It is a delicious moment of theater. Few actors would have been able to hold the freeze without adding obvious physical indications of fright. Duane McCullars, as Motel, did. A gentle laughter swept the audience. Within seconds it turned into a roar. By the time Motel was able to blurt out his line, "G-G-Good Sabbath, Reb Tevye," the audience was convulsed. He struck something in all of them and they laughed sympathetically, identifying with situations from their own lives. This was Duane's own "bit," and it was the first time he had shown it to us. An actor of less than Teddy's perception, assuming that Duane had forgotten his line, could have gone on to the next piece of business and spoiled the moment. Teddy, to my own amazement, immediately saw what Duane was doing and held the moment, giving timing leadership to Duane. This was ensemble playing in the finest sense. It augured well for the future.

After the preview performance I wrote a special letter.

TO: The Beautiful People of Anatevka, Russia
FROM: Your Czar
SUBJECT: The First of Several Triumphs

Boy, oh boy, oh boy! This was some evening. (I'm so turned on to _us_ that I can't consider going to bed though it is after midnight.) I am so full of feelings that I don't know where to begin (honest, Duane!). I guess the thing most in front of my blown mind is the regret that I couldn't get backstage to hug every one of you before you left. The parents were lined up to the back to shake my hand and compliment YOU for an exciting, funny, moving, interesting evening.

NOTES: _CHORUS:_ "Tradition" has never gone so well. It was right there (except for your careful restaging with all the Puerto Rican girls on one side and the black ones on the other—hmmmmmmm).

BEVERLY (Golde) and _OLGA_ (Yente): Gosh—I loved your scene. I sat back as if I had never seen it before and found every second of it sheer delicious. I loved what you both did to the silverware and, Olga, adding a sneaky plate-changing routine was brilliant! I loved your taking time, Olga, to make your points. I loved Beverly's reactions to your every word. She really (Beverly) made the audience aware that this was not a pure comedy scene but that something IMPORTANT was happening to the characters. This is seldom so in amateur theater—where a scene can be absorbed on several different levels. It appealed to EVERYONE in the audience—even me. The rest of your scenes, Beverly, were magic. You really manage to hold a character and thus, the audience.

TEDDY (Tevye): On the whole an EXCELLENT beginning!!! Most everyone loved "If I Were a Rich Man." I regret to say that I did not. I loved some of your timing. BUT it became a standup comedian's bit instead of a real indication of TEVYE'S WAY OF MAKING UP DREAMS. It wasn't strong enough and there was too much mugging (ham acting). I had the feeling you were saying to yourself, "Go ahead and laugh, people, because I, Teddy Smith, KNOW how funny I am." We discussed how this cuts the humor of a number in half—the knowing you are being funny. It is OK in an *Oliver!* but not in a *Fiddler.* But, I'm not criticizing you in any way. I am proud that you had the guts to try it that way. If all of it doesn't work, we just search for what does and insert it in between all that WAS excellent about the number. This is why we rehearse. The usual problem of being understood when you shouted existed. When you confront Mendel with his Bible snobbery you blow it when you should cash in on it by becoming unintelligible in speech. Shout but shout cleanly. Be careful you don't cover Motel's bit before Sabbath prayer—this is really HIS problem but you have to help him.

DUANE (Motel): Your bit about "Good Sabbath, Tevye" was sheer brilliance. You got a laugh even before you said the line. Audiences love to be able to think ahead like this. The timing was (and is) professional on this. I am still concerned about your speaking too fast. Lots of your lines were lost on this audience. It is a problem you must constantly be aware of. But you have established a wonderful, real character that is loving.

DAUGHTERS: There was so much life and energy in "Matchmaker" that I sat back and drank in every drop of your excellence. I don't like any of you EVER looking out and smiling to the audience. This is Tevye's bit and we must not steal it. Maritza really got into something and turned on lots of people from her acting INSIDE of Hodel rather than outside. Mary, remember to be last into the house bit because the number stops if they can't get around Tzeitel. Your Yente bit was superb! Carmen finally showed she has life and was a delight to watch. I loved how Dianna made something out of nothing and has gotten into the scene. Sheila, your Chava has never been better. Your voice—oh, how I wish I had more like it. You also act from inside and you warm all of us. I am so full of love for all of you.

I must sleep. Has it been worth it up to now? YES! If we had to end this project right now I would sleep like a baby knowing all is well with the most wonderful group of human beings I have ever known.

Hey . . . Thanks.

11

Interest in the production spread from New York City to the suburbs and neighboring states. My evenings were spent responding to mailed ticket requests. It should have been exhilarating. It was suffocating and I became very uneasy. It was the *idea* of a black *Fiddler on the Roof* that had captured imaginations. Professionalism cautioned that this idea alone was not sufficient nourishment to entertain and hold an audience for two and a half hours. Some segments of the show were excellent but, in general, the production was far from where it should have been in terms of goals. On Broadway, for example, transition problems from scene to scene had been accomplished by use of a revolving stage which simply moved cast and scenery on and off stage with a flip of a switch. We had no such turntable. Consequently, our cast and crew were required to execute a quasi ballet in order to get themselves on and off the set without interrupting the fluidity of the story. This aspect of the show needed constant work. One absent member could break down our human machinery. Also, with characterizations hardly set, I found myself uncertain of what to polish next.

A crucial romantic situation in *Fiddler on the Roof* involves Chava, Tevye's daughter, who eventually runs away to marry Fyedka, a Gentile Russian liberal. Against Jewish tradition, Tevye had given his two oldest daughters permission to marry men of their own choosing, without the aid of a matchmaker. When faced with Chava's request to marry outside the faith, he refuses to even discuss it. In defiance, she elopes with Fyedka. Tevye therefore declares her dead and forbids Golde, his wife, to speak of Chava as among the living. It is, perhaps, the most touching human situation in the show and, of all the subplots, given the least coverage in the script. We were in trouble with the scene.

Sheila Haskins, our Chava, was a very angry girl. Her mother was active in school affairs and her father, a baker, was eventually elected to a PTA presidency. She was one of five children. Her natural desires to be like her friends were kept in check by parental strictness. Sheila felt persecuted because of what she considered to be unreasonable restrictions placed on her behavior. She would retaliate with silence. Consequently, her development as an actress ceased. Her acting was wooden and would remain so until I thought I could make her angry enough to tell me to go to hell. I informed her mother of my desire to help Sheila bring out her gut feelings. She was shocked and exclaimed, "Mr. Piro, Sheila told us about what goes on between you and Teddy and we think it's terrible. If she opens her mouth to curse you out we want to know about it immediately. It will be her last curse."

Teddy and I now fought at least four times a week. He stood onstage and cursed while I sat quietly and took it, sometimes giving it back. It freed him. He was growing in leaps and bounds as an actor and as a young man.

Sheila, on the other hand, continued to give me the silent treatment each time I criticized her. She didn't listen to directions. She was constantly talking both on and off stage. She wore funny hats in her love scenes to make her partner laugh. She was seldom prompt for rehearsals. She was late with her entrances and missed the timing on her exits. She would not memorize lines. None of these failings represented an insurmountable problem although I exaggerated each one hoping to get her to express one real emotion, anger. Nothing worked.

Linus Sellars, our Fyedka and Sheila's love partner on stage, was equally frustrating. Linus liked to think of himself as "cool." He was an exceptionally bright young man who was not doing well academically. Studying did not fit into the image he decided to project. Fyedka was aware of the injustices of the worn-out Russian society and liked to warm himself by fringe associations with the Jewish community. He patronized their tailors and their bookbinders, and throughout the play is seen always looking in on, but never participating in, Jewish affairs. I identified with Fyedka. Linus did not.

Fyedka manages to catch Chava alone in Motel's tailor shop. She is frightened of Russians and tries to leave. He prevents it by offering to lend her a book. At first she refuses but then relents. He says, "Good. After you return it, I'll ask you how you liked it, and we'll talk about it for a while. Then we'll talk about life, how we feel about things, and it can all turn out quite pleasant."

The two scenes between Fyedka and Chava are brief but vital. Each has less than seven lines to establish a relationship. Consequently each line had to swirl with an undercurrent of emotions. Linus wasn't cutting it. His own complicated personality, which he insisted on portraying, was wrong for this show. Fyedka was not "cool." He was open, innocent, and obviously afraid of his very real emotions. I tried every technique I could think of, from addressing Linus as "Mr. Phony Cool" to working on bringing his anger into the open. All failed because, simply, he was afraid of Sheila. She was sexy, hot and cold, vixen and clinging. Linus liked us to believe he was an outstanding ladies' man, tall, handsome, articulate, and consistently well dressed. Apparently he appealed to teen-age girls, but his fear of a showdown, sexually, prevented him from acting freely. In short, he was a normal middle-class adolescent boy.

Sheila in turn played one boy against another as she did with Reggie and James, always stopping once the male had been attracted. But, to his agony, she refused to "play" with Linus. Her woman's instinct warned her that he was not then ready and she had little patience with his adolescent gropings. Linus was bright enough to know his game was not working on the one girl that mattered. He pretended, badly, to be disinterested, and projected disdain. I saw the problems and damned the lack of time which prevented my going through the psychological probing necessary to help these two children. Frequent discussions with Sheila's parents failed. They wouldn't hear of relaxing their house rules, and the thought of Sheila's shouting at me—as I desired—was abhorrent to them. Talking with Linus as we walked to the subway together barely helped.

In desperation I asked Dan O'Neil, an English and creative-writing teacher, who served as our photographer and general directing assistant, to take these two in hand and help work out the acting problems. Dan was perceptive and had a way of getting inside children. He met and coached them privately. Linus remained "cool" and Sheila silent, but through great effort Dan brought them up to the point where they were adequate as actors. Sheila functioned well in her scenes with Tevye's other daughters, especially in "Matchmaker," where her mature singing voice added immeasurably to the excitement of the number. And thanks to Dan O'Neil, she fit into her love scenes with Linus so that, at least, they retained minimal script values without ever igniting more than half the scenes' potential. Nevertheless, I seldom watched her second act moment without tears and goose bumps.

In this scene, Sheila, as Chava, attempts a reconciliation with her father, Tevye, after the elopement. He rejects her plea of "Please speak to me," and falls back on his traditions. As he dances off to the hidden chorus's "Tradition" she stands and screams, "Papa! Papa!"

Howard Enders added to the problem of Linus and Sheila. He had finally signed contracts with ABC-TV to write and direct a documentary film—*Black Fiddler, The Negro and Prejudice*—and planned on building a considerable part of the film around the mixed marriage of Chava and Fyedka.

One weekend he invited me to his home in Larchmont, a thirty-minute drive north to suburban Westchester County, in order to view a screening of the five-minute pilot he had shot of our show project. Since it was important that he have a good relationship with the cast, I asked Bruce to drive Teddy and myself there on a Sunday afternoon in late March. Howard was pleased to have this opportunity to get to know Teddy outside of school.

Teddy met me in Manhattan and Bruce picked us up for the drive. Teddy insisted on sitting in the back so, as he said, "I can sit in front of an open window." After a moment I glanced back. He was smoking a cigarette.

"Teddy," I said, "you really don't have to hide that weed. All of us here smoke."

"I know." He was embarrassed and anxious to avoid conversation about his smoking.

"So," I suggested, "why don't you just smoke like a normal teen-ager instead of sitting back there and hiding it?"

"I told you," he said, annoyed. "I like sitting back here."

"Got any more cigarettes?" I asked.

"No."

"Want one of mine or Mr. Birnel's?"

"No, thank you. Why don't you two just talk and let me look at all of these trees?"

Something was going on. My Teddy-meter indicated I was to drop the business or suffer another temper scene.

In the car going back to Brooklyn I asked, "Teddy, did you have a good time?"

"Sure," he replied eagerly. "They were great but at first I was afraid."

"Afraid of what, Teddy?"

"I was afraid they wouldn't like me."

"Do you think that's unusual?"

"Well, for a boy it is but when I grow up—"

"Bullshit!"

I turned to Bruce and said, "What about you? You're not a boy and you were meeting the Enders family for the first time. How did you feel?"

"I felt scared, I guess," Bruce admitted. "I wouldn't say anything about it if Teddy hadn't. Whenever I go into a house or meet people for the first time, I'm uptight about what they're going to think of me."

"You're not just saying that?" Teddy asked.

"Come on, Teddy," Bruce responded. "At this stage of our marriage do you think I have to resort to silly games with you?"

"All right. All right." Teddy had had enough.

"Teddy," I asked. "What's the best thing that happened this afternoon?"

"I don't know. Seeing the film, I guess."

"Do you know what I think the best thing that happened is?"

"What?"

"That Teddy, born Booker T. Smith, had the guts to admit that he was afraid. It's a little complicated to go into right now but I'm proud of you. Welcome to the human race."

We drove several miles in silence.

"Mr. Piro?"

"Yes, Teddy?"

"Can I have a cigarette?"

On Monday, Mike Wallace of CBS called while I was still teaching. After class I walked to the office. While I was waiting for a free phone, Dr. Robbins signaled me to come into his office. He handed me a letter from a daily newspaper in Jerusalem asking for a story.

I smiled. "Dr. Robbins, now we belong to the world."

He dismissed me with a disgusted wave of his hand. The pressures of publicity were annoying him. Publicity brings responsibility and he was nervous and uncertain about the outcome of so much attention. Obscurity is the fastest way for a New York City administrator to rise in his career.

"Mr. Piro," the secretary announced, "your call to CBS is ready."

I picked up the phone and identified myself. A very British voice said, "Jane Nichols here. I'm unit director for the *Sixty Minutes Show*. We'd like to do a segment of your *Fiddler* for telecast in two weeks. Now, since *Fiddler* is currently being filmed in Hollywood, the contracts state that no more than seven minutes of actual show time may be shown on the media. Consequently, we'd like to use all that time with actual performance. It won't be an interview type of thing."

"Great," I said, for lack of a better response. "What can we do?"

"I'd like to bring my crew to your school tomorrow and watch a rehearsal so that when we come with equipment we'll know exactly what we want to film. My editor will be there to get ideas for transition and sequence."

"Tomorrow will be fine," I said. My first thought was, "Damn. Another rehearsal lost for a showoff session. I'm going to have the best-publicized bomb in history." Rehearsal time was becoming precious and I hated giving up whole afternoons for publicity. Jane Nichols informed me that they would need a minimum of three hours of filming to come up with a seven-minute segment. Each child would be paid $10. We set up the next afternoon for her to see a rehearsal. It was time to stop being secretive about our two minor "improvements" on Joe Stein's script. I decided to unveil our heresies.

Early in the show, Tevye agrees to meet Lazar Wolf, the butcher, in the tavern to discuss the marriage of his eldest daughter, Tzeitel. Tevye does not like Lazar, but since Golde would be delighted to have her daughter married to the richest man in the village, the fact that Lazar is nearly three times Tzeitel's age is not a problem. Lazar arrives first. Shortly afterwards, a group of young Russians arrogantly enter the Jewish tavern. There is a moment of silence when the Jews refuse to make a table available. Perchik, the Jewish revolutionary, attempts a physical confrontation but is restrained by his friends. The Jews back down and move to the other side of the room murmuring their displeasure. Tevye comes in and notes with annoyance the presence of Russians in "their" tavern. An agreement with Lazar is reached. They sing the song, "L'Chaim." Word of Tzeitel and Lazar's betrothal spreads and they are soon surrounded and serenaded by the other Jews. Then, to their disgust, the Russians jump on a table and sing congratulations to Tevye and Lazar. The Russian song begins in derision but warms to sincerity and, in the end, the Jews and Russians join hands in a frantic dance which climaxes with a pileup of bodies, everyone laughing and sharing a rare moment of fellowship.

Joe Stein's script then calls for a blackout and change of scene as the Jews, drunk with schnapps, move outside the tavern, where they bump into the Russian Constable and are informed of a "little unofficial pogrom" within the next week. "It is regrettable," says the Constable. "But a dignitary is to pass through the village and we Russians must show that we have done our duty to our Jews."

Our script "improvement" involved eliminating the change of scenery. Instead of a blackout upon completion of the dance and pileup, we held the moment for applause. Then, in our version, the Constable walks into the tavern. He sees the confusion of bodies—Russians and Jews—and frowns in disapproval at the fraternization. Both Jews and Russians remain immobile. The Constable moves to the group, takes the Russian nearest him, and angrily grabs him by the back of the collar and pulls him off the pile. He does this again, and one by one the group separates. The Russians again look at the Jews with disdain. Slowly and silently two groups form on opposite sides of the tavern. Last to get up are Fyedka (the Russian who later elopes with Tevye's daughter, Chava) and Tevye. Fyedka offers Tevye a helping hand. From the floor Tevye looks at the hand, and then to the Constable. Ignoring the offer of assistance, he rises and moves towards the Jews. He feels somewhat soiled. The dialogue then continues from that point; the Jews are informed of the forthcoming pogrom (which eventually takes place during Tzeitel and Motel's wedding reception).

One day after rehearsing this scene, I told the company, "You know this is a change. Does anyone have any idea what we are doing?"

"I do," shouted Duane and Teddy together.

"Duane, let's hear you first. What's going on?"

"Well, that's easy," he said. "The Russians are embarrassed to have the Constable see them dancing with Jews."

"Why?" I asked.

"I really don't know. I guess the Constable is the one who really hates Jews, not the people."

"So?" I prodded.

"Well, they don't want their boss to see what they're doing."

"Why don't they get rid of the Constable?"

Olga, with an anger inappropriate to the moment, said, "Mr. Piro, why didn't *you* get rid of your union president during the strike if you disagreed with him?"

"Touché, Olga," I said, pleased. "It isn't exactly the same thing but it's close enough. What we're saying here in the play is this: we're all victims of the prejudices of our superiors."

Teddy, anxious to be heard, said, "If they would just let us alone, people would get together. They would just come together."

Jane Nichols and her CBS crew arrived on time the next day. I was becoming anxious. We had been featured on New York City news broadcasts and in the *New York* magazine. Now we were approaching a national network presentation. Jane, who was in her late twenties, wore a belted trench coat and her hair bobbed short. She impressed me as being warm and vital.

"Mr. Piro, I noticed you have scheduled the final number, 'Anatevka,' " she said.

"Yes?"

"We'd love to see it, of course, but if I remember correctly from the Broadway show, it just won't work for a televised medium. Group things seldom do, y'know."

She was asking to save time.

"Miss Nichols—"

"Do call me Jane. Janie if you'd like."

"Jane, will you suffer us an indulgence? Several times Joe Stein has offered us help."

"Marvelous."

"But I haven't accepted it."

"Good for you if you don't need it."

"Well, it's not exactly that we don't need it. It's that we've made only two changes—alterations, actually—in the script."

"Oh?"

"I blew several opportunities to talk to him about it."

"Even though he offered?"

"Yes. But he's Joe Stein and I'm Mr. Nobody. One change is in the number, 'Anatevka.' I would really like you to see it and give me your candid opinion."

"I'd love to. Carry on."

Janie's crew consisted of seven men plus her editor. They quietly took up places throughout the empty auditorium. I moved to the tape equipment in the pit and called out, "OK, Bruce. We're ready when you are." The house lights dimmed. We showcased "Tradition," "Matchmaker," the Yente-Golde opening scene, "L'Chaim," and "Do You Love Me?" The children were totally professional in moving from scene to scene in spite of the broken sequence. The CBS crew quickly caught on that we enjoyed and expected their vocal approval of each piece of business. They laughed and applauded heartily. What began as professional courtesy from CBS quickly turned into genuine affection. The children rose to the occasion and gave magnificent performances.

Now it was time for the big number "Anatevka." This is a quiet, gentle song sung by the Jews as they reminisce about their little village. It is sung as a farewell to the only life they have known, in response to the news that Moscow had decreed the territory cleared of Jews. When the Constable informs Tevye of the news "as a friend," there is the first hint of Jewish resistance. Tevye orders the Constable off his land, as long as it still is his land. Russians and Jews move in for a confrontation. Again, the Jews back down. When alone, they panic. So much needs doing. In just three days they must liquidate their assets, separate, and go to different places around the world.

The script calls for a quick exit of the villagers, leaving only Tevye with his family and closest friends on stage to sing "Anatevka." The song, one of the foundations of the production, indicates the historical strength of Jewry and their ability to remain intact as an ethnic group.

Rather than making a quick exit, as written, our villagers moved to the front edges of the stage in small groups, went down the outside stairs, crossed the pit, and moved up the auditorium aisles while singing. Each villager was to take someone from the audience, very quietly, and ask, "Will you join us? We must leave now." They then continued singing and moved in procession to the back, with their guests, to remain for the last three minutes of the show. During this exodus, two remote-controlled films were projected, covering both auditorium side walls. These films, shot by Dan O'Neil and Bruce, showed a slow-moving snowscape synchronized to give the observer the sensation of walking slowly through a winter forest. Throughout the color film, three-second black-and-white cuts of tenement buildings from the school neighborhood were subliminally inserted. On stage the family grouping remained stationary in the pose of an antique photographic portrait. Lights were adjusted in sepia to further heighten the effect.

I was watching for CBS reactions when something drew my attention to the stage. I turned. Tears were rolling down Teddy's face and he was making no attempt to stop them. The cast sang, "Soon I'll be a stranger in a strange new place, searching for an old familiar face." Teddy was seeing nothing. With eyes front he was pouring fourteen years of experiences into the moment. His makeup had streaked and part of his beard was in his hand. I waited. He didn't move. The number ended in silence. He was out there in Anatevka.

He blinked. After a moment he became again Teddy Smith, comic, and broke the tension.

"Sheee-it!" he exclaimed.

We howled.

"That's it, gang," I called. "Go back to the prop room and get undressed. And no kissing or biting. Any costume or prop or piece of makeup I find on the floor or anywhere else it ain't 'sposed to be will cost you ten dollars. Performing is just a part of show business. Move!"

The sudden thought of ten dollars cash revived energies, and they started for the prop room.

"One more thing," I began.

"We know," Beverly said. "Get ready for notes on the show."

I ignored the suggestion. They waited, poised. When the tension was greatest I whispered, "Thank you."

Janie was standing behind me, wiping her eyes. The camera man next to her was blowing his nose. The rest of the CBS crew were looking at me, at each other, and at the retreating cast with awe. I heard someone say, "That was the most moving experience I have ever had in a lifetime of going to the theater." Janie dug into her purse and came up with a handful of money. "I'd like as many tickets as this will buy and I'll send you a check for more."

For the next ten minutes they were ecstatic in their approval of the experience, especially "Anatevka." As film people they were excited with the visual effects, something that had been seriously lacking in the Broadway production. Eventually we got down to business and discussed what was to go into the seven-minute film for the *Sixty Minutes Show*. It was pouring rain, so I hitched a ride home with Jane.

That evening my phone rang. It was 11:30 and I was surprised since my friends knew that I didn't answer the phone after 11 P.M. I picked up the receiver.

"Hi, Dick, this is Bruce."

"Hi, Bruce. Wasn't that incredible today?"

"Yeah. Listen, I stayed till about ten tonight and most of the lights are hung."

"That's fantastic! I was really worrying about your finishing them. So tomorrow we start working the crew for the other special effects?"

"Right. Oh, by the way, I got membership in your club."

"What club?"

"I got mugged tonight." He said it simply as a statement of fact. Bruce was never an actor and did not underplay for effect.

The next morning I got to Dr. Robbins' office early and as he entered I told him about Bruce's mugging. His face froze as he went into a short speech about our recklessness in remaining in the neighborhood so often alone. He knew we knew the risks and was angry that we chose to ignore them.

When the children assembled for rehearsal that afternoon I again related the incident.

"Mr. Piro," Beverly said, "why do they always pick on the teachers who put in so much for us? Why don't they get the gang that run out every day three minutes after the last bell?"

I had no answer.

12

Spring weather arrived and with it the collapse of the New York City school system.

Most of our graduates went on to Canarsie High School, a mammoth institution twenty or so blocks from Junior High School 275. At that time the ethnic breakdown of Canarsie's four thousand students was twenty-five percent black and Puerto Rican with Italian-Americans making up the majority of the seventy-five percent white population. During the previous summer, 1968, Brooklyn race riots involved armed confrontation between blacks and the Italians who had formed a mock organization called SPONGE (The Society for the Prevention of Negroes Getting Everything). Eventually we began hearing of incidents where black pupils were waylaid and seriously beaten by Italian vigilantes. Black children were in terror of going to or from Canarsie High without escort.

In Junior High School 275, five percent of the student body was white, almost all Jewish. These Jews were quiet, frightened, and anxious to avoid attention. It didn't work.

Younger brothers and sisters of the Canarsie High blacks decided to avenge the wrongs going on up the street.

One such incident involved David Farber, a meek, frightened eighth-grade honor student. As he left our building one afternoon, he was momentarily separated from his friends. He was instantly surrounded by a crowd of blacks and beaten unmercifully. He was overweight and offered little resistance. The spectators, as silent as the assailants, gave no vocal warning to the teachers who were passing enroute to their cars. The mob then lifted David's bleeding, unconscious body and attempted to impale him on the spikes of the iron fence surrounding the school. Luckily, he fell over the locked fence. Attempts to scale it were thwarted by the staff that by then had been alerted. David was rushed to a hospital. Shortly afterwards his family moved out of Brooklyn. We never learned if he recovered.

I was horrified and related the incident to all my classes. This event had occurred in view of hundreds of children, none of whom made any effort to stop it. The children were unwilling to hear me out and insisted on their rights to take revenge wherever they wished. They stubbornly refused to acknowledge a difference between a militant Canarsie Italian, surrounded by compatriots, and a single, quiet Jew. Characteristically, they saw only white.

The situation worsened. Race riots forced Canarsie High to close several times in the next two weeks. During this period, gangs of "liberated" high-schoolers descended on our block and forced their way into the building by threatening children who refused to open side exits. One afternoon fifty outsiders were discovered in our cafeteria organizing a general walkout. It almost succeeded.

To protect our white students, we were forced to keep them segregated in special rooms. They ate lunch in a classroom rather than run the risk of eating in the crowded, explosive cafeteria. After the incident involving David, they were dismissed early so that their parents could escort them home. These precautions further angered blacks who objected to this obvious preferential treatment.

Parents, fearful for all pupils' safety, demanded that Dr. Robbins chain the outside doors with the exception of the main entrance, which was guarded by black adult school aides. He refused. It was against fire regulations. Since the custodians would not jeopardize their positions without written orders from Dr. Robbins, an impasse was reached. Parents threatened a boycott.

They warned the principal that unless he chained the doors to protect the children, they would not send their youngsters to school.

Dr. Robbins finally gave in to combined community pressures. The doors were chained and special keys given to certain teachers who were to use them in the event of a fire.

As race riots spread, more high schools were closed. Radical high-school student demands were taken up by the junior highs. These included:

1) Discontinue general courses [a non-academic, fill-the-time curriculum for projected dropouts].
2) Unlimited class cuts with no penalties.
3) Freedom to move through buildings without passes.
4) Improved school lunches.
5) Automatic permission to leave buildings for lunch periods.
6) Elimination of all police from school property.

Activists, adult and student, infiltrated our building to rally support. In a Brooklyn high school, a teacher who challenged admission of a stranger into his class was doused with fuel and set on fire. Assaults against teachers became daily occurrences throughout Brooklyn. Police would call, warning, "There are three gangs roaming the streets and headed your way." Both teachers and students began carrying concealed weapons for self-protection.

The two days following the chaining of the doors were quiet. Teachers relaxed. However, there were new rumblings from within. Beverly Cannon, our Golde, took the responsibility of organizing a faction of angry students.

"Look, kids," she said at a lunchroom meeting of seniors, "we have a great school and we like it. Now, I agree some things can be better. Why don't we do it right and go see Dr. Robbins and talk to him about it?"

They listened and selected a committee. With Beverly at the helm there was no cause for alarm. Amelia Brown, the assistant principal, was delighted at the students' ability to institute democratic action. A delegation went to the general office with Beverly as its spokesman.

"What do you want?" a secretary demanded.

"Ah, we'd like to see Dr. Robbins, please," Beverly asked, politely. (It was common knowledge that his office was open at all times to parents, teachers, and students.)

"Do you all have passes to be down here?" the secretary challenged.

"Yes."

"Well, he's very busy but I'll ask him anyhow."

Abruptly Beverly was shoved aside by Clarence, a six-foot student with an Afro haircut, who placed himself in front of the secretary. He had little to lose, for he had been bypassed by the system and it was almost certain he would, upon reaching sixteen within a few months, become a dropout. He was unable to read, and spent most of the schoolday in the halls shaking down smaller students for nickels and dimes. All disciplinary action against Clarence had failed since most teachers were in physical fear of him. He was allowed to move freely in the building. Many of the staff felt he should have been placed in a special institution since ours was unable to provide the proper psychological help he required.

"Look, bitch," he snarled. "We wanna see Robbins and

we're gonna see him now, y'hear? Go in there and tell him we're comin' in."

Beverly tried unsuccessfully to maintain leadership. The students were exhilarated by Clarence's daring. They loved a fight and urged him on.

Dr. Robbins overheard the threat and refused to see the children. He would not be pressured into meeting anyone, least of all a group led by Clarence. Ignoring Beverly's frantic pleas for rationality they left the office and headed towards the lunchroom, hoping to start a walkout. A crowd gathered as students poured out of the cafeteria to join in the disruption. With swelling ranks they continued chanting and marching down the corridor. Two teachers were spotted rounding a corner. The crowd gleefully changed their direction and rushed to another floor gathering still more forces. There were then over a hundred boys and girls laughing and running from floor to floor. For most it was a holiday, a game. Pupils who tired of the "demonstration" found escape impossible. They were forced to keep up with the mob or risk being crushed. Panic drew a gentle breath and then exploded through the ranks. Outside doors were chained. The main entrance was guarded. There was no way for them to get out. Momentum eventually slackened but not before some pupils were hurt, several classroom windows smashed, bulletin boards ripped off the walls, and Dr. Robbins overrun in his attempt to stop the children.

An unidentified person phoned an outside activist group, reporting that the students of Junior High School 275 were being chained inside the building "like animals." A general cry went up to take the chains off the doors or else. Parents and teachers pleaded with the children, trying to make them understand that the chains were there for protection and not imprisonment. Reason went unheeded. An organized gang of high-schoolers systematically stoned the building, breaking all second-floor windows. Black students, victims of flying glass and bricks, cowered under desks and in closets. They were confused. Why were their black "brothers" hurling stones and metal junk at *them*?

The mayor responded to our cry for help by sending a task force of three bearded black men to meet with student leaders, listen to their grievances, and, hopefully, restore order.

Dr. Robbins was stunned. "I can't believe it's personal," I said.

"Of course it's not personal," he replied.

"Then why our school?" I asked.

"Because," he said, "the other schools around us went down the drain years ago. If they can destroy us then whatever remaining schools are functioning will go down like a house of cards. It's the best they're after, not the worst. They've been looking for a crack in our walls all year. The chains gave it to them."

"What do you think they really want, Dr. Robbins?"

"To destroy."

"And then what?"

"That bridge will be crossed when they come to it."

"Do you have any idea who 'they' are?" I asked.

"That's the worst part. Leadership changes from moment to moment. As soon as we meet and reason with one group, another begins agitating somewhere else. It's slippery. We just can't get hold of anyone that has the respect of all the kids. The ones who scream invective the loudest at that moment—those are the leaders."

The mayor's special task force met with students around the clock. The primary ingredient of their technique was boredom. They met and met and met. The thrill of conferring with a mayoral task force in the principal's office was dampened by the third hour. However, because of shifting leadership, this boredom technique failed.

Beverly Cannon was enlisted to speak to the eighth grade during a lunch period. The class, some six hundred children, gave her momentary attention as she outlined some of the privileges of being a senior. When she mentioned that those privileges, such as a prom and graduation ceremony, might be rescinded, she was shouted down. She fled the podium in tears.

Throughout the riot days I tried to assume a business-as-usual attitude. After-school rehearsals were run in a battle-zone atmosphere. Students came immediately from their last class to the auditorium. Doors were then locked, with a student guard posted at each entrance. I wrote to cast parents and assured them that, as long as the children were with me inside the auditorium, they were safe. No one was allowed to enter or leave. The most dangerous situations existed in the streets immediately following general dismissal. Since it was unreasonable to ask teen-age boys and girls to go from an 11:10 A.M. lunch period to a rehearsal ending at 4:45 P.M. without refreshment, I broke a school regulation and allowed selected students to leave the building one hour before dismissal to buy food and drink for the rest of the cast. Once we closed the doors they remained shut. The auditorium became an oasis in a desert of violence.

Agitation continued and became part of the "natural" pattern. Subconsciously we adjusted to it as we had to excellence and as we had to violence and as we had to failure year in and year out. Automatically we ceased using certain "dangerous" stairwells and specified bathrooms. No teacher or pupil dared walk close to the building, under the windows, for fear of being hurt by thrown debris. Firecrackers tossed into crowded stairwells became routine, except to those who lost sight or hearing. Events that would have been catastrophic a week earlier became hardly worthy of discussion.

One such incident involved the *Fiddler* set. Student painters from the art department, who were about to put final touches on the scenery, had foolishly left buckets of paint on the stage. Vandals took those buckets and splashed each piece of scenery, the floor, the curtains, and the piano, which was then pried open. Hammers were ripped out and the keyboard smashed with an iron pipe. Tevye's milk wagon, an antique we had purchased from a truck farmer, was rolled across the stage and thrown into the pit. Dr. Robbins and Bruce were disgusted. I tried to understand. Certain students wanted desperately to become part of our excitement. Due to low academic achievement they knew they would never be part of those drama activities which made our school prominent, since performers in music, drama, art, and creative writing were drawn from the better classes. Because they could never get involved constructively, they destroyed what they could not join. We tightened auditorium security and started set-painting over again. Another music teacher was relieved of teaching assignments for a week and repaired the piano. Rehearsals went on.

Along with student disorders, Howard Enders and the ABC crew caused serious disruptions.

"Dick, I've just got to have two days of shooting this week," he insisted.

"Howard, I've got to rehearse." I exploded.

"But we just need a few shots."

"Howard, we made a schedule and I've got to stick to it. I'm going to have the best-advertised bomb in history."

"What are you talking about? The show looks great."

"To *you* the show looks great because the only things you've seen are the things you're filming. Of course those scenes are great. We've done them a million times for you and for CBS. What about transitions? Characterizations? What about training the technical crew with runthroughs instead of showcase scenes? What about the cast moving smoothly from scene to scene? I'm sorry, Howard. I've got to think about my show and my kids and my audiences."

"It's a shame," he said. "You were coming out so great. When this thing hits the network you'll be—"

"Howard, you're blackmailing me again."

"How dare you say that?"

"Because every time you ask for a block of time not on the schedule and I refuse, you bring up the fact that you're going to make me a star and I'm not helping you."

"That's a ridiculous thing to say."

"Howard, you're blackmailing me."

"I won't even listen to that."

"Howard," I explained, "if being a star means I have to ask an audience to pay good money to come and see four or five good scenes sandwiched between boring, unrehearsed, dull, meaningless shit, then I have to say to you, 'Go fuck your stardom.' I've got a job to do. If your part destroys my entire show then *you've* got to go."

"OK, Richard. I'll try to make do with what we have."

The next day I received a frantic call from Howard.

"Richard, you're not going to believe this," he began.

"Try me." I was cautious, used to his deviousness in achieving his ends. We were cut from the same mold.

"Well, the last day's shooting was ruined in the cooker."

"The what?"

"The temperature of the developing fluid was off. Hundreds of feet were totally destroyed. What are we going to do? Without that footage we have no film."

I gave in, as usual, and Howard descended for another grueling session. A shooting session involved several "performances" of a single scene, done first with stationary cameras placed in the back of the theater. The same scene was repeated with cameras placed midway. The cameras would then move into the pit. Finally, portable cameras were used threading in and out of the cast as they performed. In order to give Howard absolute freedom to cut and splice, each performance had to be exactly the same.

The children performed their best and then flopped down on the stage floor to rest between takes. The excitement of hearing a sound man call, "*Black Fiddler.* Take three. Roll 'em" quickly turned to boredom. My task was to revive the children and keep them at peak performance. It wasn't easy and there were days when I resorted to sarcasm and cruelty to keep up the children's efforts.

Teddy, on the other hand, never lost interest, and did some of his finest work for Howard. He was a star and he knew it. Special efforts were made to keep Teddy happy, since the success of the film, as well as the show, rested largely on his frail shoulders. Howard did his best to keep the children functioning by providing sodas and other refreshments during the long hot hours of filming. Since he refused to allow any of us to see rushes or portions of the film, the most obvious motivation for the children was removed.

Dr. Robbins became anxious over the constant presence of the "dreaded media" in the building. My assurances that the ABC crew had contracted to film only the show—not anything else—fell on deaf ears. During one of the most serious student riots, the film crew left the auditorium, without equipment, and went outside to observe. A gang of blacks was again stoning the front of the school. Thirteen police cars and a solid row of policemen were parked just behind the vandals. Howard, reacting to the wanton destruction, went to the officer in charge and screamed,

"Why are you standing here like this?"

"Orders," the officer snapped.

"Orders? But they're destroying municipal property. Behind those windows there are little boys and girls hiding from flying glass and bricks. How can you just stand there doing nothing?"

"Mayor's orders," the officer replied through clenched teeth.

"But as long as you stand here doing nothing, what's to stop these hoodlums from setting fires?"

"Look, buddy, move on. You might get hurt standing here."

The following days brought countless bomb scares. Several high schools were again closed. Students had planned mass demonstrations at City Hall. Bomb threats were used as an attempt to close the junior high schools and give younger students freedom to join the rallies. It didn't work. We ignored the threats and tried to run a normal school.

I was frantic for rehearsal time. A letter was sent to Robbins requesting that Bruce be relieved of all regular teaching assignments in order to work with his light crew. It was denied. Consequently, in addition to ABC and Howard, I had rehearsal competition from Bruce, who needed the stage as desperately as I did. If he couldn't work on the stage, we would have neither lights nor special effects. He got the stage.

Before the disorders I had felt safe promising Jane Nichols a three-hour block of shooting time during the last week before opening for the CBS *Sixty Minutes Show*. However, we had not counted on riots, among other things. Since Howard had been coming and going at will, I didn't consider the CBS date important enough to tell Dr. Robbins. He had enough to do in coping with the disorders.

Exactly on schedule at 8:30 A.M. on Wednesday, several white trucks with large CBS insignia painted on the sides pulled up to the main school entrance. Crowds gathered to watch the men unload equipment. Since it was a lovely spring day, most of the seventeen hundred children in the school had, as usual, come early to chat and visit in the schoolyard before the 8:40 entrance signal. The CBS unit was an exciting distraction. Dr. Robbins looked out his office window and panicked. "TV crews and rioters mix like Kool-

Aid and water," he said, running outside. He held up his arms and shouted, "You cannot come in here."

Janie Nichols arrived in her car.

"Dr. Robbins," she said, "we have a signed statement here from Mr. Piro. This filming date was confirmed."

"I don't care what you have. I'm principal and I refuse to allow you to enter this building."

"Dr. Robbins," Janie pleaded, "this is going to cost CBS thousands of dollars."

"I am in deep sympathy with CBS's poverty," he scoffed.

"But a special crew was flown in from the West Coast just to do this shooting. According to union regulations they must be paid whether or not we film."

"You are not gaining admission to this building," Robbins insisted.

I dared not intercede. The CBS unit turned back. I was deeply embarrassed. No matter the details, blame for the situation would be placed on Janie. She was so in love with our show and our kids, the thought of her suffering from it professionally was intolerable. Several phone calls were made and another filming date set for after the opening, if we ever did open. She rightfully demanded assurances in writing that CBS be allowed to enter the building. Robbins agreed with reservations. To avoid crowds the crew must arrive after school was in session. Secondly, the trucks were not to park near the main entrance and—especially—all CBS personnel were to arrive in small groups through various side entrances. CBS accepted Robbins' conditions.

Three days before opening night, Dr. Max B. Myers, the district superintendent, ordered our building closed at three o'clock in order to calm the situation. All after-school programs were canceled. No student or teacher was allowed to remain in the building. My problems were solved with ABC and CBS. We could not rehearse.

Fortunately, we had put on enough showcase performances of scattered scenes so that the children had no difficulty with costumes and makeup. They knew their prop room functions and performed them with minimum confusion. However, we had yet to do a complete runthrough. Bruce's work had paid off. We had a show that was visually stunning. Bruce had completed hours of work on enough individual light dimmers to require a backstage crew of thirty boys, some running single spotlights which, due to power limitation in the main light board, had to be hooked up elsewhere.

Nevertheless, Bruce and I felt a sense of doom with the announcement that the building would be closed. I was convinced that the cast would deliver an excellent performance at the opening, but I could not guarantee lighting and special effects. The last days of any show, professional or amateur, belong to the technical crew, who cannot begin functioning until everything is hung, draped, painted, screwed, plugged in, and rehearsed. They are miracle workers, forced to accomplish complicated moves with minimum practice time. Without a well-trained technical crew, we had no show.

We were sold out for three of the four scheduled performances covering two successive Thursday and Friday nights. Hundreds of people from Manhattan, with no school connections, had purchased tickets by mail. Magazine and TV publicity had generated an unprecedented amount of interest in the show. Joe Stein had forty invited guests. (Due to a student's error in affixing the correct postage, his tickets never arrived and I had to send another batch.) And this was the point—three days before opening night—when we desperately needed time to pull the hundreds of details together, details that had been meticulously worked out over a six-month period. We had to have a runthrough of the entire show, followed by several technical rehearsals and a final dress rehearsal.

Bruce delivered the news about the closing of the building while I was straightening out the prop room.

I said, "At least we'll be spared another day's agony of wondering if the last bomb scare was real and praying our kids won't be murdered on their way home. Closed? No re-hearsal? Let them eat shit. This community has earned it."

13

Thursday, May 1, 1969. Opening night was exactly twelve hours away. The 8 A.M. subway train pulled into the Rockaway Avenue station. A final quick glance through *The New York Times* revealed a paragraph buried on page forty-nine relating that Junior High School 275 had been the focal point of three days of student rioting. I started down the steps thinking, "That's some way to attract an audience." I heard a sound behind me and turned. It was Nancy Gallagher, an English teacher.

"Hi, Nance. Why so early today?"

"I don't know. I couldn't sleep so I got up and washed my hair. Then I decided to try it your way."

"Your hair?" I asked.

"No, stupid, having coffee before my first class."

We walked on in silence.

"Are you nervous?" she asked.

"Yes and no. Did you know we haven't had a runthrough or a dress rehearsal yet?"

"I heard. What are you going to do?"

"Beg Robbins on my hands and knees that if they close the

building today he allow me either to have a runthrough or else to get the kids out of morning classes and do the whole thing right away before the riot."

"Do you think he'll go along with it?"

"No."

Again silence.

At 8:10 A.M. we punched in. Melvin Rose, a math teacher and office assistant, was standing behind the counter. I steeled myself. Melvin got the daily gossip first and delivered it fresh-killed to the incoming staff. His extra duty assignment was to man the telephone and arrange for substitutes in the event of teacher absentees.

"You gonna do the show tonight, Piro?" he asked.

"Sure. Why shouldn't I?"

"You mean you didn't hear?"

"Hear what?"

"Wow. Where have you been all night?"

"On the phone with my cast."

"I bet."

"Look, Mel, get it out and stop playing with me, huh? What do you think you heard and how does it affect me?"

"OK, Piro. The militants have informed the district office that if their demands are not met by three o'clock this afternoon they will destroy this school with fire and bombs tonight when you open your *Fiddler on the Roof*."

He smiled as he delivered what he thought was crushing news, then waited for my reaction. I turned, walked across the hall, unlocked the prop room and dropped my gear. I needed coffee, but the thought of facing the rest of the faculty was more than I was willing to take. I locked the door and set about unloading makeup-removal supplies: toilet paper, tissues, lard, cold cream, alcohol, soap, washcloths and sponges. I would think about Melvin's news later. Bruce arrived carrying two steaming cups.

"I knew you'd be in here," Bruce said without a smile.

"Melvin Rose just had an orgasm telling me about your reaction to the bomb-threat business."

"But I deliberately did not react."

"That's not the way he's telling it."

"As we say in *Fiddler,* 'May he have his own personal plague.' "

"He already has—his mouth."

I paused for a moment. "Bruce, what are we going to do?"

"Is that our decision or Robbins'?"

"You're right. You know what?" I'm not going to give Robbins the slightest hint of a personal choice. If he feels we should do the opening we will. If not, we won't."

"Come on, Dick, you know you won't be able to hold back."

"I swear to God, Bruce. No help from Piro this time. I will not take the responsibility of making a choice."

"You really don't care? I mean, after all these months you have no recommendation for tonight?"

"You hit it. At this moment I honestly do not care what happens to this school, this show, and—most important—this goddamned community."

"Listen to last-minute-change Charlie."

Bruce sipped his coffee in silence, staring at the room clutter and shaking his head. Finally, he turned to me and said quietly, "You've been a monster to the kids, you know that?"

"Bruce, the only way I survived these last weeks was to throw so much energy into this show that I didn't have time to think of the forces at work against us. The show, Bruce, and nothing else. Right now, if it were a question of losing one prop or the library through fire, I'd say burn the library but leave me the prop. The kids? I've tried to keep their focus on the show too. I've been driving them towards perfection so they won't have time to lose faith in the project. I think they appreciate it. If not now, they will later."

"What about the kids? Melvin said you were on the phone with them all night."

"I don't know. I suspect they're going through a hell worse than ours. We go home at night, eventually, and we're safe. I'm sure they know ten rumors to our one. They know the people destroying their world and they know the actualities of danger. We don't. I think they're scared and angry."

"Did they tell you this?"

"No."

"Then how—"

"Would you believe our conversations concerned their telling *me* to cheer up? Telling me to be calm? If an atomic bomb ever hits this city," I said, "ghetto kids will make it. They start basic survival tactics as soon as they can walk, perhaps sooner."

Bruce went into the auditorium. By the time I joined him there, he was on top of a ladder which was being held by two crew members. I noticed a third student hovering in the shadows of the wings. He was a senior, about sixteen years old, and wore a perpetual frown which I found intimidating, as he intended it to be. I didn't know his name and due to his height and breadth I was cautious.

"Are you on Mr. Birnel's crew?" I asked politely.

"No."

"Then what are you doing here?"

"I just wanted to see what was happening."

"Well now you've seen it. Nothing's happening. Would you please leave so we can get our work done?"

Rather than using the stairs that led off the stage, he pulled a typical intruder's device and tried to pass me, cross the stage, and run up the aisle shouting curses. I put my hand to his shoulder and tried urging him towards the nearest exit.

"Get your hands off of me, man," he threatened.

I continued pressing his shoulder. "Then you'll leave the way you came in?"

"Get your fucking hands off of me."

I released his shoulder and held my hands high, indicating I meant no harm. He made a quick move to get past me. This time I grabbed both shoulders hard and flung him down the three side steps. I was upon him before he could recover his balance. He was ready to fight. I pushed him the few feet towards the door.

"Get the fuck out of here," I screamed. "The next time I'll break your neck, hear?"

Before he could respond I shoved him out the door and slammed it shut.

"Wow, Mr. Piro, are you uptight," exclaimed one of the crew.

"Bruce," I gasped, "do you really need these beautiful kids?"

"No," Bruce responded, "I'm done. Thank you, boys. Remember to be back here right after lunch for the runthrough."

"Runthrough?" I echoed.

"Yeah." Bruce smiled. "Robbins gave us permission to take the whole afternoon."

"Thanks for letting me know." I started for the exit.

"Where you going?"

"To round up the cast and spread the news."

"Don't. Robbins said not to. He was in here while you were on the phone. He wants to make the announcement himself over the public address system. He also doesn't want to give the gorillas time to organize and break up the rehearsal."

I hesitated in indecision. Tommy Pringle, the student who had taken major responsibility for painting details on the set, walked off the stage and approached me in the aisle.

"Mr. Piro?"

"Yes, Tommy."

"It's going to be a great show. I can feel it."

"Thanks, Tommy. If it is, part of the blame goes to you for your fantastic art work. See you after lunch."

He left with the other boys. Bruce lit a cigarette. I sat down to think.

"What's up?" Bruce asked, after a while.

"Bruce, do you know what's happened? Do you *really* know?"

"Try me."

"Those motherfucking sons of bitches in the community, that's what."

"What are you talking about?"

"We've played right into their hands. We walked right into it."

"What are you raving about?"

"Don't you see it?"

"See what? Come on. The bell's going to ring and I've got a class."

"We took an ordinary junior high school, you and I, and placed it on the map. Why?"

"Because of the show."

"Not because of the show, Bruce, but because of the *idea* of the show. None of these people saw our *Oliver!* or *Romeo and Juliet* or *Scapin* or *Taming of the Shrew*. They expect the typical giggling junior-high-school chorus, crepe-paper costumes, brown butcher-paper sets, mothers waving to kids, cast peeking through the curtains, and maybe three spotlights, one amber, one blue for nights, and one white. They haven't the faintest idea of our kids' depth."

"So what's wrong with that? We'll deliver."

"I know that and you know that and the community knows that. And that's why we're going to be bombed tonight."

"I'm not following you."

"We're being crucified not because we haven't done the job. They'll destroy us precisely because we *have* done the job, beyond even their wildest dreams. What if we quit, Bruce? What if we just walked out right at this moment and closed the door for good?"

"I'll see you later," Bruce said, starting for the door.

"You know," I continued, "we rose above mediocrity and earned the scorn of our colleagues. I used to say, 'Screw them. It's the kids and their parents I'm after.' Well, baby, the parents are just as bad. Yes, I know the community is as victimized as we are. But, dammit, let *them* get off their behinds and get rid of the gorillas in their group."

"I've got to go," Bruce persisted, and left the auditorium.

At 9:05 A.M. the seventh-grade General Music class assembled. Calmed by a tranquilizer, I realized that I had not given thought to a lesson plan. We had been analyzing trio form through Haydn symphony minuet movements. I opened a record album and drew out the Brahms Hungarian Dances. This was a very low-level class in reading. However, their ears were incredibly sensitive to musical nuances and they could easily detect differences in musical structure.

"I'm going to play one piece through," I announced. "It takes only seven minutes. Listen to it and please don't start jiving when the gypsy melodies turn you on. Afterwards I'm going to ask three volunteers to come to the board and do the A B C analysis of the form. If they get it right, we'll spend the rest of the period on your rock records. Agreed? OK. Remember it's a fourteen-minute lesson only if you cooperate."

They listened attentively, restraining their natural inclination to respond physically to the rhythms of the Hungarian Dances. Three students immediately "volunteered" by rushing to the board. Their analysis was letter-perfect upon one listening: ABA-C-ABA. I made a ridiculous mock accusation.

"You kids stole my Brahms album and went home and listened and did the analysis. It's foul play. The deal's off."

The class was tickled and demanded two more chances to do perfect analyses before soul-record-playing time. I gave in. The subsequent lessons were also letter-perfect. Mike Cheikes, the assisting music teacher, scratched his head in amazement. He approached the phonograph and whispered, "What are you doing? Don't you know these kids aren't supposed to be able to do this kind of thinking? It's dangerous. You're fouling up the whole academic structure. These kids are supposed to be dumped from learning in two years. How can you dump someone who knows Brahms?"

I was proud and pleased. Thoughts of that evening's opening were forgotten. The morning passed quickly. One by one the cast checked in once again to give me little assurances that all would be well.

At 11 A.M. Dr. Robbins announced that the building was to be closed directly after lunch except for the cast and crew of *Fiddler*. Several teachers were assigned to help me patrol the outside areas around the auditorium until we had everyone inside and the doors locked.

At 1:05 P.M. the cast assembled. Teddy asked, "Costumes and makeup, Mr. Piro?"

"No, Teddy. Stand by the prop room and see that the kids don't go in. They are to come directly into the auditorium and sit down. No ball playing or running around. Kill them if you have to, but watch their throats. We need those."

They sat, cowed by the amount of technical activity going on onstage with Bruce and his crew. Some were obviously scared to remain alone in the building.

"Gang," I began, "this is important. Today's rehearsal is not a dress rehearsal."

"What?" Reggie burst out. "But you said and I told my mother that—"

I ignored the interruption.

"Your charming 'friends' outside have seen to that. This is probably the only show in history that is opening to a sold-out house without a dress. It is, however, a *technical* rehearsal. We'll do a complete nonstop runthrough."

Duane grinned, "I'll bet you five dollars you stop at least five times during the first scene, Mr. Piro."

"Thanks, smartmouth," I said. "If you had five dollars I might take you up on it. But I'm reading you loud and clear. I'm going to try to do it nonstop. For better or worse you are ready to do this show tonight. But, the greatest actor-singer-dancer in the world is only as good as the amount of light on him. You've all had months of work. These crew boys on stage now have had—not even days. They're getting minutes to dress and light your show. Do not—repeat—do not stop no matter what you hear me or Mr. Birnel scream. It will usually be something like, " 'Throw on switch number three, you dumb mother, and stop watching the show. Your eyes are on the script or the light switch and not on Beverly's left t . . . toe.' "

Squeals of laughter. The tension relaxed. The crew felt very masculine and very important.

"There he goes," Beverly sighed. "Using me as a sex symbol again."

"You would prefer, Miss Beverly, another symbol?" I asked.

"Hell no!" She laughed.

"OK. Places, everyone, for the top of the show. I'll see you in exactly two hours and twenty minutes."

I was stunned. The technical crew outdid the actors in excellence. Beyond one or two missed light cues, the show went through without a breakdown or even a pause. Bruce had trained a master crew. Cast members were "up" and doing their best work. The rehearsal went nonstop.

At 4:15 P.M. the cast was dismissed.

"OK," I said to them. "I've got lots of notes but I'm going

to save them for makeup. Remember, I want the complicated makeups here by six-thirty: Lazar, Teddy, and the Rabbi. Please, please do not talk to these three boys until they are completely done. They're going to hold on to all the makeup and no one is going to get glue or hair until they're finished. Teddy, thanks for hiding the new bottle of latex glue in the fiddler's violin case. We found it."

"Shit," he grumbled. "Now I'll have to find a new place."

"You do that, star, and you'll go on minus your ears."

"But I never can get it when I need it."

"If you'll come in on time and finish your job then the other boys won't be grabbing for your stuff. I tried giving you a whole set of your own and you lost it. What else do you suggest? Losing another set? Discussions of this type, this late, are a royal drag."

Teddy was angry and about to go into a tantrum, but was stopped by a chorus of disapproval from the rest of the cast.

Olga asked, "Are you sure we're going to open, Mr. Piro?"

"Olga, I'm not sure of anything except that we are ready to open. Beyond that shouldn't interest me or you. You've all heard about tonight's threats. It's up to Dr. Robbins and his boss, Dr. Myers, to make the decision. I promised them we'd stand ready and we are."

"But—" Olga tried to continue.

"I think it's a waste of time to go into 'buts.' Now, for heaven's sake, go home and go to bed. Not the sofa but into underwear-and-under-the-covers bed. Save your voices and your energies. We did a risky thing by performing on the day of an opening. You need to gain back your strength. The first person who bugs me tonight with stupid questions such as, 'Did you see my costume?' or 'Do you think the show is going to be good?' will be forced to spend three hours alone with Beverly chained to a wall."

"Who'll be chained, the person or Beverly?" asked Duane.

"That might not be a bad idea. She has that look in her

eye again, and maybe the prop room won't be safe with her loose."

"Come on, Mr. Piro, I'm tired," Beverly said.

It was time to go.

"Fun and games begin here at seven tonight. God bless you. If I'm not here, do have a lovely time."

They bounded out into the street. Bruce moved to adjust several spotlights. I sat trying to decide whether it was wiser to put on my tuxedo before going across the street to eat or whether I should wait and dress with the cast. A knock at the back of the auditorium revealed the face of Roland Brown, a former student who had turned militant. I started up the aisle to let him in.

"Hey," Bruce warned. "The building is supposed to be cleared. Don't open it."

"Look, I'm the one who's supposed to be jittery. It's Roland. Remember? He's the kid who was my assistant-on-the-payroll in the Title I Drama Program two years ago. I think he's a senior in high school now."

At the same moment Dr. Robbins and Superintendent Myers appeared on stage and asked to speak with me. I let Roland in. "Can you wait a minute, Roland? Dr. Robbins wants to talk to me and I haven't seen him all day. Let me get rid of him and we'll chat. We open tonight and I don't have to tell you what kind of work that leaves me with until tonight is over."

"Sure," Roland agreed. "I'll sit here, OK?"

I moved on stage, out of earshot, and greeted Dr. Robbins and Dr. Myers.

"Dick," Dr. Robbins said, "we've decided to go through with the opening tonight."

"Thanks for the good news. When I didn't see you today I assumed the green light. What prompted the decision, or shouldn't I ask?"

"Because," Dr. Myers replied, "not to go on would be worse

than going on and we were forced to take the lesser of two evils."

"Dick," Dr. Robbins inquired, "do you know anything about the rumors concerning the teachers?"

"What rumors?"

"I've just had a call from the Brownsville Community Council. They're convinced that these student disorders have been agitated and perhaps even started by the Jewish teachers in order to stop *Fiddler.*"

"That's ridiculous," I said.

"It's not ridiculous," Robbins replied. "True or not, what's of vital importance is the fact that the community believes it. Our only answer—our only weapon—is to go on as scheduled. Are you ready?"

"Yes."

"Good. What time are the children reporting?"

"The first wave will hit the beaches at six-thirty."

"I don't like the allusion, but I'll see you then."

Dr. Robbins and Dr. Myers turned to leave. I called to their backs, "Hey boss, enjoy the show. It just may be the last."

Robbins tried to look stern. "Your gallows humor is out of place," he said, and continued out of the auditorium with Dr. Myers clucking behind him. I felt giddy, convinced that we were on a collision course. We would open. It was enough. Robbins and Myers were in a very tight spot and on the verge of panic. Good. Let them now taste some of the frustration and agony we had known every day for the past six months. I jumped off the front of the stage and moved into the seats where Roland was waiting, expressionless.

"What's happening, Rolly?" I asked.

"Mr. Piro, I only have a minute."

"So take a minute. You're entitled."

I looked closely at this young man. With his almost blue-black complexion, high Afro hair style, embroidered African dashiki, belled pants, studded sandals, and sunglasses, he was the embodiment of the new Afro-American, proud and strong. He had been the best improvisation student I had ever had. But our close relationship cooled the day I mistakenly asked him to read aloud from a script with the rest of the class. He had a quick, sharp intelligence. To my surprise I realized that he couldn't read and had compensated by developing an impressive vocabulary and a sharp wit. He was then finishing high school and looked forward to college entrance on an athletic track scholarship. How was he managing to graduate with sublevel reading ability? It was one of the riot ultimatums. His high school curriculum was such that if he put in a certain number of hours he would graduate through the "General Course." Academic achievement was not considered. Attendance was. The system had failed Roland. He was doing a superhuman job of trying to overcome his prison of ignorance. His blackness might have held him back up until then. This same blackness now represented his only hope for escape.

"Mr. Piro," he said, nervously, "my boys and I were talking yesterday and we decided that we liked you and we want to help you out."

"That's very nice—I mean, that you like me. I thought you decided this two years ago when we shared the teaching of an acting class."

He ignored my response.

"Now about the threats that have been made—I mean, the bombings tonight. If you give me fifty—no, twenty—tickets for tonight I'll ring this theater with my boys and I guarantee you things will stay cool. Now, if not . . ."

His voice trailed off as he shrugged his shoulders. Part of me screamed, "Tilt!" The other part of me considered his threat just one more installment of the nightmare. Fire, bombs, and destruction if I don't release tickets. Law and order if I did.

"Roland, you know we're sold out?" I stalled.

"Come on, Mr. Piro, all you have to do is put your name on little slips of paper. We're not particular."

He stood up, stretched, and faced me squarely. He had been hesitant at the beginning of the conversation. Now he was confident his plan—whatever it was—would succeed. Part of his new blackness required absolute rejection of gratitude based on acts committed by a white. He was testing himself more than he was me.

"Roland," I said, quietly, "this is blackmail."

"You don't have to take that attitude, Mr. Piro," he said, quickly, trying to make the threat in his tone cover the sudden fear.

"What attitude do you suggest I take? Have you any doubt about what you're doing?"

"I—"

"I could go into a long thing about the year we spent working together. In fact, that particular improvisation class graduated the guts of tonight's cast. It's what's going to give tonight's show that extra bit of excellence. I would hope you could have felt you were partially responsible for it. I would have been delighted to give you a complimentary ticket, two, in fact, so that you could have brought a date."

"Well, if you want to . . ." His eyes lit up.

"I want to but I won't. You took a risk, my 'friend,' and you lost."

Bruce appeared on the stage and shouted for me to get ready for dinner.

"I will not give you twenty tickets, Roland," I said. "I will not give you even one because, unlike your friends, parents, and relatives in this jungle, I will not be blackmailed by you or any other pseudo-savior of your people."

He seemed ready to leave. I went on. "I will be in the pit tonight working the sound track in full view of the audience. It is approximately twelve feet from the nearest outside exit.

You go ahead and bring your boys to mess up the house. Within three seconds, maybe shorter, I will be in a car headed towards Manhattan. I won't even turn back to see the smoke. I leave you a building filled with your soul brothers and sisters. So, my friend, mess away and you're welcome."

Bruce was getting impatient.

"Look, Roland," I said. "I've got to go. Thanks for the visit. Hope you manage to get to one of the performances. You won't regret it. And, by the way, I appreciate how desperately you wanted to see the opening. Next time just ask. I don't have to tell you that this conversation never happened. We've got too much love behind us to let this moment spoil what may be ahead. And I do love you, Roland."

He put his head down and slowly walked away. As he got to the door he turned, lifted his chin and sent me a look that started chills at the base of my spine. I held his stare. Furiously he opened the door, passed through, and slammed it shut. My feeling was that I had moved us closer to the brink.

At 5:30 I donned my tuxedo, locked the auditorium, checked the makeup areas, and started across the street where Bruce had gone to wait for me. I slid into the booth, ready for a drink. Bruce and I felt caught—doomed—by the inevitable, and we chatted meaninglessly, afraid of facing the major issues. The door swung open and a group of cast members filled the center tables. This was most unusual since the restaurant was far out of the students' price range. I signaled to Teddy. He came over.

"What's happening, Teddy? Why are you all here so early?"

"We went filming with Mr. Enders."

I went blind with fury and asked, "Where is he now?"

"Oh, he went home to get his wife and kids."

"Who's going to pay for your dinners?"

"Mr. Wilderson, the unit director. He's in the bathroom now. Yeah. He's got the job of feeding the troops."

"Thanks, Teddy. Just be across the street in an hour for makeup, OK? Don't make me drag you away."

As Teddy left Bruce murmured, "That's really foul play. What a rotten thing to do. The kids must be exhausted."

"God bless the media, Bruce," I said. "They're good to the last drop—of our blood. He knew I wouldn't permit any filming today so he didn't even bother to ask. Instead, he hid out there somewhere and kidnaped the kids."

"I wish we'd thought of it before and warned the cast."

"Bruce," I said, "I hope Enders gets caught in the worst traffic jam in history trying to get back here by overture time."

"Well, there's nothing we can do," Bruce said. "It's over. Let's just hope the kids have the reserve energy they're supposed to have. They all look high. Hope it lasts."

At 6:25 we finished eating and started across the street, accompanied by some cast members who had noticed us through the glass windows and sheepishly responded to our invitation to share a soda. I let the children into the prop room and went into the auditorium for a last-minute check of the sound track. The first thing I noticed was the ABC crew setting up filming equipment in the pit. They had moved out some of the chairs of the school orchestra—which was to play the overtures—to accommodate microphones. I ran down the aisle shouting.

"Oh, no, you're not! Out! *Out!*"

"Look, Richard," Norman Wilderson, the ABC unit director, began.

"I told you months ago that I will absolutely not permit filming during the show. *Fiddler* is much too delicate a script to overcome the glamour of TV lights and cameras. I want that audience to be totally with the cast and not half with us and the other half wondering when it's 'going to be on.' "

Wilderson pleaded. I held firm. Howard Enders had not yet arrived. If it had been he I was confronting I might have persisted. The crew's "assignment" was to film the audience entering and then get a one-minute sequence of applause. We had simulated an opening night several days before but they needed a real audience to make it stick. Wilderson pledged the filming would be inconspicuous.

"We will not use bright lights," he promised. "We won't disturb any aspect of the show in any way."

I was too strung out to argue effectively. Reluctantly, I gave my consent and went to the outside door to clear the entrance of the rest of the cast.

At 7:00 P.M. I walked around to the front door and saw Dr. Robbins confronting a police officer.

"You absolutely cannot remain in view of this audience," he shouted, on the verge of hysteria.

"Mr. Robbins, we have our orders from the station and, as I see it, we are on duty for the duration of the performance."

"Do you know what will happen when certain factions of this community walk by and see fourteen squad cars parked in front of the school?"

"Well . . ."

"I'll tell you. Their honor will demand a riot. Every dreg in this neighborhood will arrive with a rock to throw. TV crews are expected. Then we will have all the ingredients for a very nice party—an angry community, massed police, and instant publicity. I won't have it!"

A system was worked out. For the duration of the evening, thirty-five officers were to remain hidden on the second floor in readiness. They would maintain constant radio contact with the auditorium. Several other policemen were to fan through the building. Only four were to remain in view of the audience during the show. Two would man each exit and several were to patrol the outside areas surrounding the school. Later I heard the chief ordering his men not to remove a single piece of their equipment. They were to remain in such positions that, if needed, they could appear within seconds of the alarm.

I reported these events to Bruce and several members of the cast during makeup. As new children arrived the word was passed and exaggerated until, according to their story. half of New York City's vast police force was present upstairs, and some hinted that the National Guard had been called out.

By 8:00 P.M. the auditorium filled rapidly. There were no reserved seats and people wisely arrived early. I had little to do. The children were, by this time, professional in preparing themselves for performance. Making up was a matter of routine and they had long ago been conditioned not to go onstage, not to peek into the audience, and to remain quiet until they were due to perform. Bruce, who was in and out of the house, reported the presence of the dignitaries—Harold Prince, Joe Stein, Sheldon Harnick, Jerry Bock, producer and authors of the show; Margaret Henderson and Joan Scott, prominent New York theatrical agents; the United Nations Human Relations group; Shirley Rich, casting director of the original *Fiddler*; the WBAI crew preparing for a subsequent broadcast; the executive board of the Brownsville Community Council; some members of the Board of Education; plus many "dubious types" of show-business people. Occasionally Dr. Robbins and Dr. Myers appeared, nervous and exhausted, with Amelia Brown trying to assure them that the audience was calm. They were a self-appointed roving patrol. Dr. Robbins was proud of the fact that our shows went off smoothly. They were among the few school activities which he, his wife, and sons could come to and enjoy. Tonight he had no intention of calmly sitting back and watching.

At 8:15 P.M. I gave Mike Cheikes, our school band director, a signal to start the overture. I edged through the clarinet section and took my seat near the sound equipment in the center of the pit. *Fiddler on the Roof* was seven minutes away from opening at the Harry A. Eiseman Junior High School 275, Brownsville, Brooklyn.

14

The gold curtains parted. Out of the darkness, needle-thin drawings of yellow and green birch trees were projected on the backdrop. As the trees receded into the distance, the fiddler's theme was heard. Over suspended housetops a tiny pin spot picked up Anthony Holland, the fiddler, nonchalantly playing his tune. Teddy walked through the side pit door, up the stairs, and into position on stage left. For a moment he watched the fiddler, amused and tolerant. He turned towards the audience and began, "A fiddler on the roof? Sounds crazy, no?"

As he approached the end of the monologue with, "That I can tell you in one word—tradition!" the main house revolved off the stage and the ensemble, led by Reggie on one side and Beverly on the other, made their entrance. Tall and proud, they danced on in two files singing "Tradition." The house broke into thunderous waves of applause. Cast chins tilted higher.

The audience continued to applaud every gesture, every double take, every comic routine. They were approving both the ideas and the execution. This was our first experience with viewers who were predominantly professional. They were letting the entire production staff know that no piece of work was going unnoticed. The cast was obviously buoyant.

As "Tradition" ended the ABC cameras swung towards the audience and focused on the Haskins family, an obvious unit complete with an infant child asleep on Mrs. Haskins' lap. Blinding floodlights illuminated the auditorium, breaking the spell of the show. The Haskins family was filmed every time the audience reacted. I was numb with fury but helpless because I could not leave my post without stopping the show.

Act I ended and so did the filming. During the break between acts, the cast found places in the prop room where they rested. Makeup was adjusted. The children were surprised and pleased. Script situations that they had long taken for granted were getting strong vocal reactions from the audience. Several youngsters exclaimed, "I didn't know I was so funny." Olga was characteristically trying to analyze the electricity that had flowed between cast and audience.

I looked for Teddy. He was lying on a folded piece of scenery, obviously exhausted. I was concerned. During Act I he had pushed his voice beyond his normal capacity. His timing was a shade off because of the need to catch his breath. He was working hard, too hard for the character.

Maritza, our Hodel, had gone into a Puerto Rican-movie style of acting. Each of her lines was fraught with tragedy and was preceded by a sob. It threw me, but later I learned it worked well for the audience. Beverly had been absolutely perfect and stood as a rock for the rest of the cast. The first act had been slightly down from what I knew was the ultimate potential of this cast. Given the circumstances, including a first runthrough that afternoon followed by a grueling filming session, it was still a major miracle. The technical crew had performed with stunning perfection, not a light cue missed.

Later we learned that a group of black militants had appeared outside the building with rocks and bricks. They had sporadically stoned the school during the first act. The police kept the audience inside during intermission, thus avoiding a confrontation.

Act II, in general, was closer to our potential than Act I. During the final minutes following "Anatevka," Tevye's close friends came to say good-bye. Yente and Golde chatted and, as usual, Yente clowned, hiding her real feelings. A casual farewell was exchanged. Yente, the matchmaker, was on her way to Jerusalem and Golde was leaving for Chicago. Just before Yente disappeared from sight Golde froze and gently called, "Yente?" The tragedy was in blinding focus. They fell into each other's arms, touching, looking at, and feeling each other for the last time. Behind me, in the audience, a woman was sobbing, "I knows it. I just knows for that woman."

It was over. The cast had marched down the aisle singing "L'Chaim" and up onto the stage for curtain calls. We had prepared three. The audience was on its feet yelling, stamping, and keeping rhythm with the music. Beverly frantically signaled for me to come onstage. I ignored the gesture. Finally Teddy joined her and together they came down into the pit. I followed them back to stage center. Floodgates of emotion opened and the entire cast and crew burst into tears. They were all over me, hugging, kissing and pulling at my clothes. They were hysterical and the conditioned-teacher part of my brain flashed, "Caution." They had lived with the fear of violence for twenty-four hours a day, and few of them had truly believed the show would go on. With infinite kindness they had kept these feelings of doom away from me. I had been unaware of the depth of their hopes for this show until I saw them sobbing unashamedly on stage. Now, at last, they could give in to their feelings.

I signaled for the curtains to close, but Dr. Robbins leaped on to the stage and held the children in place. He spoke in a restrained tone for the next twenty minutes, praising the cast and crew. I couldn't understand it. Normally he was a man of few words who firmly objected to principals giving speeches at student performances.

Later I asked him about it. "Dr. Robbins, believe me, I'm not complaining or criticizing, but what were you really doing with your speech?"

"Congratulating you and the kids, naturally."

"No. I don't buy that, although I'm grateful."

"Well, what else did you think I was doing?"

"I think you were concerned over the audience."

"What do you mean?"

"You were afraid a turned-on group of people would combine with a volatile cast and pour onto the streets. The resulting spontaneous combustion might precipitate a riot. So, you bored them into submission. They left orderly and peacefully."

"Did I do all that?" he smiled.

"Yes, you did. And you know it."

"Well, if you say so, Dick."

I was never absolutely sure.

The cast did not wait to see me after opening night. There was no need. They had done exactly what they were trained to do and more. Characteristic of black ghetto children, they did not require constant adult adulation. When they "rang the bell" they were content. It was enough. By the time I got backstage most of the children had left. I got out of my tuxedo and went to join some friends for the car ride home.

That night I wrote a letter:

TO: Cast & Crew of Lovely Fiddler on the Roof
FROM: A Has Been
SUBJECT: Opening Night, May 1, 1969

It's one o'clock in the morning and I'm numb but trying desperately to come up with an overwhelming comment about tonight. I think this letter is a mistake and it makes writing that much more difficult. The one word which keeps knocking at my brain about you is--"respect." I think you have come through with quality theater under the most, most difficult of circumstances. You know, I gave up this week. I broke under the combined pressures of Fiddler, the student unrest, and the #)$)%(¢* ABC film crew. I was prepared tonight for total failure which means--and I'm ashamed of this--that I gave up on you. How silly of me! I still can't believe you did what you did. I guess I can't get my usual thrill out of it because I feel that you did it in SPITE of me--which means I feel sort of left out.

I find it nearly impossible to believe that this project is on the way to becoming a brilliant page in the history of Eiseman Junior High School. After every production I generally have a feeling of peace--a feeling of a job well done--a sense of "let's get on with more things." I don't have these feelings now. I can't let go of Fiddler and yet--I feel a degree of pain which tends to wipe out the feelings of joy connected with a production that has been so extraordinary as this one. On the other hand, there is YOU.

You are the first group that I picked three years ago and literally handmade for this production. No other bunch of students could have done it. I have been investing all I've got in you for so long that it is most painful for me to let you go. Letting go of Fiddler means letting go of YOU. That's what teaching is all about but every year at this time it destroys me--instead of getting easier to bear.

If I teach for another 100 years I will never again get involved in a project that covers so much of what I believe teaching should be. This show drew blood, and maybe in a few years I will tell you just how much damned trouble it caused with students, teachers, parents, and politicians. I wish I could say that I knew what the outcome would be. I can't. I had that deadly feeling that, since I had won all the other battles over the years, I was due for a failure and it would be a big failure. I hadn't counted on you and people such as Lil Carter, Frances Brown, Dr. Robbins, Mrs. Amelia Brown and Bruce Birnel. These people will henceforth be known as "The Patron Saints of Fiddler on the Roof."

Remember, our primary purpose was to give our school and our community a damned fine piece of theater. Lots of things changed in our school. Lots and lots of people have different ideas about blacks, and Jews, and human relations. Why? Not because we delivered a message but, rather, because we gave them the best show the town has ever seen.

For hundreds and hundreds of people--this show will never close. They (and maybe us?) will constantly refer to it because it opened our eyes to many things. If the word "mazeltov" has become a permanent word in your vocabulary we have been a success. It is not my purpose here to list what has happened as a result of Fiddler but one of the most exciting things to myself and a certain few other teachers is the fact that our community (school and home) now share our views--no, not on Jews and blacks--but our deep belief that the boys and girls of our school are FIRST-CLASS CITIZENS OF THE WORLD AND ARE CAPABLE OF DELIVERING FIRST-CLASS CONTRIBUTIONS TO SOCIETY. Lots of people think they believe this vital fact, but when the ABC and CBS things hit the air they will not only really believe it but will start acting on that belief. Remember--there are various kinds of poverty and only ONE of them deals with money. The others deal with poverty of the spirit, poverty of ambitions, poverty of good feelings about yourself.

I have to end because I feel like preaching what I no longer have to preach to you. Go in good spirit. You have done an incredibly good job. The love and respect I am feeling for each of you (even Duane) is tying up my tongue. I know it's corny, Beverly, but may I reprint some of the Sabbath Prayer?

> May the Lord protect and defend you.
> May the Lord preserve you from pain.
> Favor them O Lord,
> With happiness and peace.
> O hear our Sabbath prayer.
> Amen.

And that prop room better be so clean you can eat off the floor when I get in tomorrow.

EPILOGUE

Fiddler on the Roof was presented four times, as originally scheduled. Requests for subsequent showings were denied in spite of vehement community objections.

"We've fulfilled out basic obligations," Dr. Robbins explained. "Anything more would be madness, given the explosive conditions in this community."

A week after closing we learned that Teddy and Beverly's applications to the public High School of Performing Arts had been turned down. My meeting to plead their cause with the chairlady of the drama department proved more like a confrontation. She proudly announced that she had not reversed a decision to reject an applicant in over twenty years.

"Mr. Piro," she began, "I'm very happy to meet you. I've a casting call for a Broadway musical which is perfect for your Teddy Smith. I'm sure he'll get the role." (The show failed to receive sufficient financial backing and was canceled.)

"If you're so certain," I asked, "then why isn't he good enough to enroll at your school?"

"Well, Mr. Piro, he just isn't our kind of pupil."

"I don't understand. You saw his audition?"

"Yes. And I also saw him on TV. He's a very talented young man. He passed the audition, granted, but so did many other children. We simply had to make a choice from all those who passed. We don't have room for Teddy." Over my attempts to interrupt she then relayed the statistics of the hundreds of children who auditioned and the few the school could accept.

"I'm not interested in the other hundreds," I persisted. "I'm interested in Teddy Smith and Beverly Cannon."

We argued. Finally, due more to feelings than fact, I sensed that Beverly and Teddy had not displayed sufficient humility at the prospect of studying at the High School of Performing Arts.

"Madam," I pleaded, "each of these youngsters has had national coverage several times on television and in magazines and local newspapers. An entire performance was broadcast over an important radio station. Why should they be humble? How could they be humble? They're pros and you ask them to get all soft inside at the prospects of rubbing shoulders with amateurs? They've been trained to be proud of their abilities, not ashamed and 'humble' about them."

"I'm sorry, Mr. Piro, they're just not *our kind* of student." The interview was over. I was dismissed.

At this point, Harold Prince, producer of the original *Fiddler on the Roof* as well as *West Side Story, Damn Yankees, A Funny Thing Happened on the Way to the Forum,* and *Zorba,* wrote to the school stating that he had seen the children's work and believed in their ultimate value as professionals. That failed. He then contacted members of the school's honorary board of advisors (a glittering array of leading show-business personalities) requesting their help. She refused to budge despite their appeals.

Dr. Robbins went through official channels, finally reaching the second in command at the Board of Education. They failed. Frances Brown of the Brownsville Community Council marshaled all her forces. They failed. Teddy and Beverly graduated and went on to Canarsie High School to pursue a normal academic course.

As the term ended, my request for a medical leave of absence was granted. I planned on finding an island upon which to reflect, and recuperate. It was my energies and directions that needed healing, not my ulcer.

The June parting with Dr. Robbins was bizarre, with his insisting, and my denial, that I would never return to J.H.S. 275.

"Dick," he said, "no one who gets away from a situation like ours ever returns. Mark me. In retrospect things here will seem worse. You won't be back. Good-bye."

Then there was no question in my mind. I would return.

Six months later, in November, I learned that Dr. Robbins had voluntarily transferred to a new public junior high school in an untroubled, white, middle-class section of the borough of Queens. His immediate assignment was to supervise the final construction of a building and work out a program for the incoming classes. It was an enviable position and one sought after by most principals in New York City.

During the six months' leave I had been corresponding with several students. Beverly Cannon was then going through a crisis of racial identity. She had suddenly discovered nonblack popular music and was being ridiculed by her friends for having "abandoned" her black soul.

"I still dig soul music," she wrote, "especially when I want to dance but the words of acid rock groups really turn me on when I feel like just listening. I mean they really speak to *me*. And I'm not trying to be white, honest. You've got to believe me."

I did believe her. Intellectually she was ready to fly out of mental ghetto boundaries. Her friends, left behind, were jealous and were making Beverly pay for each of her steps into adulthood. Our correspondence grew to a letter a week.

Several eighth-graders, still in the school, wrote letters articulating their hurt and resentment that I was not in Brooklyn to see them through their senior year of dramatic glory. Each plea to return brought pain. It had been difficult for me to leave the children. It was easy to cut short my stay in Greece.

Amelia Brown, who was appointed acting principal after Robbins' transfer, was overjoyed to hear that I intended to return to work at the beginning of the second semester and start rehearsals immediately for a belated production of *The Crucible.*

My return in February was greeted in the faculty room with hostile remarks concerning Howard Enders' film, *Black Fiddler, the Negro and Prejudice* which had been nationally telecast by ABC on August 7. Most teachers felt the film had dug up old hates since Howard had successfully portrayed black anti-Semitism. Our production of *Fiddler,* they charged, was simply an idea upon which to hang a larger picture of prejudice. I, too, was disappointed with the lack of full coverage given to the children in the film but felt that Howard had succeeded brilliantly in what he set out to do, to expose black as well as Jewish bigotry. Deservedly, the film later won the Robert F. Kennedy Memorial Award for excellence in television journalism. I was proud of it and him.

Since I had not been expected back for the following academic year, those children who had trained with me for two years beginning in their sixth grade were dispersed and frozen into programs which did not include music or drama. Thus, for the first time I found myself with a drama class at Harry A. Eiseman consisting mostly of total strangers. They were honored by being in drama and demanded the traditional rewards but were unwilling to work for them. Unlike previous senior drama classes, they had not had the opportunities of watching a production grow from the first groping reading through the ecstasy of an opening night with the months of sheer labor in between. Neither had they shared in the group experiences in Somerset, Massachusetts, with the choruses. They acted within the normal limits of their observations; you were chosen for drama and you became a star with special academic dispensations.

The worst offenders were the few graduates of *Oliver!* and *Fiddler*. They refused to be turned on by *The Crucible,* knowing somehow that it was manipulative (since I expected it) and we were in the age of no more manipulation from the white establishment. They were rude to me and ruder to one another. My push for a personal relationship was met by a wall of distrust.

The year before only Teddy refused to "perform" without an audience. The following season, the entire cast refused to put energy or invest feelings into rehearsing. When it was too late to recast, the leading lady began two months of blackmail.

"Janet, where were you yesterday?" I asked. "I called home and your mother said you'd gone to school."

"I was at my girl friend's all day."

"Then you were truant, right?"

"Right."

I steered her into the office to phone home.

"You call my mother," she cautioned, "and she'll take me out of the show. Then you'll be really stuck. I promise I'll come in for rehearsals even when I don't come in for the other classes."

Calvin Jones, who played the male lead said, "Why should I work? Nobody else does. Get off my back."

The ensemble declared, "If the stars won't do any work, why should we? They get all the glory, anyhow."

General Music classes, which comprised the bulk of my teaching program, were a disaster. The music teachers whom I replaced had given up and had been playing popular records throughout each class. The music room had turned into a black discotheque. This was the one class children now refused to cut. It was more fun to riot in the music room than roam the halls.

The physical condition of the building was deplorable. Stairwells were permanently marred by great splashes of paint on the tile walls. Litter spilled down the stairs in surrealistic patterns dimly illuminated by broken light fixtures. Char marks in corners indicated where fires had been set. The odor of human defecation and urine hung over the corridors. Hall clocks leered through broken, twisted faces. Sometimes we inhaled chemical Mace sprayed by hostile students. Such incidents occurred so frequently as to be unworthy of lunchroom conversation. Several times a week doors were flung open and stink bombs or firecrackers or brilliantly colored smoke bombs were thrown into classrooms. Children shouted in glee as they moved to the windows for air. Those who failed to escape the fumes simply smiled, unwilling to show anger. Resistance had become useless. The hallways were filled with children screaming, laughing, shoving, smoking, running, or dribbling basketballs. This behavior pattern generally spilled into the beginnings of each class. Teachers began reporting senseless violent confrontations with students.

"Would you please take your seat? I'm ready to start class," I asked an eleven-year-old boy one morning.

"No," he answered sullenly.

"What do you mean, no? You're not sitting?"

"No."

"Fine. You have my permission to leave class without a penalty. I have a lesson to teach and I can't do it with you standing between me and my class."

"No."

"You refuse to take a seat and you refuse to leave, right?"

Silence. There was absolutely nothing left to do outside of physical violence.

"You have three counts to move." Rapidly I counted to three then quickly grabbed the child and shoved him out the door, which I then shut and locked before he had time to begin the usual stream of invective. It was a trap and I fell into it time after time. Some teachers felt that these children were being taught to let no opportunity for confrontation pass. Readily I began using physical force to keep minimum order. The students listened to no other language. There seemed to be no other way. The first time a teacher resorts to force he has finished his usefulness.

One day, I chose the relative quiet of midperiod to go to my classroom to set up equipment for showing a film strip. On the stairwell I encountered three children from the seventh grade, each twelve years old. The girl was lying on the floor, her clothing pulled up above her waist. One boy was kneeling on her shoulders. The other boy was penetrating her sexually. It was not rape since she was obviously enjoying herself. I paused, shocked, and waited for them to scramble up and move to another spot in the building. They continued as if I were not there. Stupidly I asked, "Just what do you think you're doing?" The young lady twisted her head to meet my eyes and said, "Man, if you don't know at your age maybe you should stay and watch." I retreated down the stairs and took another route to my room.

Out of a group of thirty-two drama students, five were special. At least two of them took turns spending entire days by my side. I loved these special children. More important, I needed their obvious affection to serve as a filter for the hostility of the others. Adding to my guilt was the fact that these children were hurting academically by spending so much time away from their normal classes.

On March 25, 1970, at 3:14 P.M. during a stage rehearsal of *The Crucible,* a sophisticated incendiary device was set off in the prop room. We lost everything. The entire *Fiddler on the Roof* production was destroyed. We had carefully stored our costumes and sets for a possible performance in Los Angeles. (Through the ABC telecast, a group had extended an invitation for an all-expense-paid trip.) In addition, we lost our collection of over nine hundred costumes, all properties, scenery, scripts, photographs, tape recordings of past performances, records, books, and most of the lighting equipment. The morning after, Bruce and I faced not only three feet of gelatinous rubble but the knowledge that special steel cabinets had been ripped open and their contents stolen by the firemen. Thus we lost cassette tape recorders, all of Bruce's photographic equipment, lenses, cameras, extension cords, and other small items which seemed of value. Only Bruce and I were shocked to learn of this "official thievery." Members of the community and the students laughed at our ignorance of life in the ghetto. The attitude of the police was, "Well, what did you expect? They risk their lives. Soldiers loot, don't they?" We spoiled any chance of retrieving the equipment by making an official claim for the loss.

No official comprehensive investigation was made, nor was it requested by our community. It was of small value to realize why ghetto residents stone firemen.

One week later, Bruce Birnel's office was set on fire. Quick discovery prevented another catastrophe.

Throughout the remaining few weeks of school, kerosene was poured on the stairwells outside of the second-floor music room. Several other attempts were made to light fires. Open doors at the bottom of the stairs prevented the fumes from building up and the attempted arson failed. In desperation Amelia Brown gave in to student demands and authorized permission for all children to leave the building during lunch. As anticipated, this new freedom made it easier for more children to go truant, and an afternoon calm was thus established. No children, no trouble.

On May 21, 1970, *The Crucible* opened for a single performance. (The remaining scheduled performances were canceled since all schools in the city were ordered closed by the Board of Education to quiet the city-wide student unrest.) We needed a miracle to pull the show together. Typical of the fantastic inner resources of children, we got it. The cast performed magnificently. Once again Bruce Birnel came up with stunning visual effects. But the audience ignored comic moments in the script and the biggest laugh occurred during the last moments of the show when the hero is hung by church authorities for refusing to sign a false confession to witchcraft. There wasn't a moment's silence throughout the evening. Gangs of high-schoolers paid their dollar admission and came prepared for a party, complete with paper bags filled with refreshments. The show never had a chance. Raucous laughter that was unrelated to stage action, rolling beer cans, exploding firecrackers, and the sound of transistor record players counterpointed the work of the cast. Frequently the actors were required to play with heads turned aside due to the rain of paper clips shot from elastic bands. We dared not stop the performance. It was obvious that a riot had been planned for the evening.

Children who were scheduled to be in the next year's drama class had been working backstage for *The Crucible.* They looked at me angrily.

"What's the matter, Dennis?" I asked the boy who had been precast as Don Quixote for the following season's *Man of La Mancha.*

"You think I'm going to work every day after school and on weekends for an audience like this?" he said. "I wouldn't give them shit and no one else will, either. Get used to it now, Mr. Piro, and save yourself a lot of screaming."

In anticipation of possible disruptions we had printed an urgent request for parents asking their help in supervising the students in the audience. Every parent present had received a copy. The request was ignored. Adults were displeased with the students' noise but they made no move to improve the situation. During the performance I pleaded with groups of high-schoolers, "What have you got against this cast? They've slaved for months to provide this evening's entertainment. They're the only ones suffering from your rebellion. How do you hope to 'get the establishment' by getting them?" My appeal succeeded for as long as it took to approach another noisy group.

I remembered the spring production four years earlier. That night seven hundred people jammed the auditorium which seated six hundred and remained spellbound by a production of *Romeo and Juliet.*

After the performance of *The Crucible,* I waited for parents to comment upon the recent prop-room fire and offer either assistance or sympathy. They came to say hello. The multiple fires weren't mentioned.

One week later our Spring Concert started an hour late because a predominantly adult audience refused to come to order and allow the string orchestra seated on stage to perform their opening selections. In disgust I left the microphone where I had been pleading for attention and moved to the outside ticket table. Standing there were several black school aides and Amelia Brown. About thirty children from six to eight years old, attracted by the free activity, tried to gain entrance. We reiterated the rule that concerts could be attended by little children only if they were accompanied by an older person. Despite our rule, children no more than seven years old crashed past the guards and stood a few feet away taunting, "Can't catch me, white motherfucker!" They were fearless and we were powerless.

In June we tried something new. School was dismissed early for the purpose of having a grand faculty-community meeting. Several panels were set up, including discussions on sex education, drug addiction, curriculum planning, discipline, reading problems, and sensitivity training. Teachers were assigned to attend a specific panel and parents were free to go where they wished. At the end of two hours, participants were to return to the library for a report from each individual panel leader.

After panel meetings the library was filled to overflowing with people sitting on every available space including window sills, desk tops, and stacks of books. I was perched on top of the librarian's desk at one end of the rectangular room. Having just come from a sensitivity-training group, I was feeling open and free and loving.

To my surprise, Mrs. Diaz rose and asked the assembled teachers which local board they intended to support, the one recently legally elected or the opposing defeated slate which was calling for a new vote and going from door to door extorting housewives. It was obviously a planted question totally irrelevant to the business at hand. The teachers remained silent.

Then a black man of about thirty-five rose slowly from his seat near Mrs. Diaz. He slowly surveyed the group. Then with a deep gravel voice began, "I'm a black man, see. I was planning on shaving off my moustache and beard but now I'm glad I didn't because it helps you all to see that I'm a man. And I'm black. If that isn't clear enough to convince you then look a little closer."

His tone turned more derisive as he continued.

"Now, I assume some of you out there might have gone to junior high school sometime in your life. Maybe some of you even went to high school, since you're teachers. Now, perhaps a few of you might even have gone to college because—"

At this point I broke. Feeling that only I could do what needed doing, I slammed my hand down on the desk and screamed with all my strength, "Goddammit, say what you mean, man, and can all this damn crap!"

"Who are you?" he demanded.

"The name's Piro and I'm chairman of the music and drama department and I don't need your hostility."

"I'm saying all you teachers are fucking idiots!"

He started towards me. As he moved, three men fell into step behind him. Everyone remained motionless. I leaped to my feet, more frightened than I had ever been. Suddenly the man's path was blocked by Olivia Stukes, the black gym teacher who had assisted in the direction of *Fiddler*.

"Go ahead," she jeered. "Kill him. Do the nigger thing, baby, 'cause that's how we act. I mean, don't talk, don't reason, don't discuss, just *off* him. He criticized you, didn't he?"

Jim Contrada, the assistant principal, was trying to get the now-volatile room into control by shouting my credentials to the angry parents, who were refusing to listen. Amelia found me and said, "Dick, will you come outside?"

"Amelia," I said, "I'm perfectly calm now. Don't worry. I'll apologize. If I go outside with you they'll think you ordered me to apologize. Then it won't work."

"That's exactly what I want," she said. "I want them to see how well I control my staff."

I shrugged at such logic and followed her outside. She had nothing to say. We paused a moment in silence and returned inside the library. As I shut the door a woman leaped up and pointed an accusing finger in my direction.

"That man has no right to be in our school," she yelled. "If he can't control his filthy mouth in front of a group of parents just imagine what he's like in the classroom. He's corrupting our children's minds. I demand his removal immediately."

She was quickly joined by another black woman and together they continued to berate my foul language and demand my dismissal. Most of the parents shouted their agreement.

Some of the staff remained frozen with the horror of the situation. Others, who had missed Mrs. Diaz's question, were trying to catch up with the sequence which led to this open fury.

As the women shouted and Jim Contrada attempted to regain control of the meeting, I paced in the back of the room, partially out of sight. Teachers I approached refused to acknowledge my questioning expression or invitation to comment. Parents turned their faces aside. Mrs. Sara Lytch, a black parent and strong supporter of our school, approached me from the side and said quietly, "You'd best stick by me, Mr. Piro. I'll see you to the subway."

Eventually the meeting resumed. The anger had subsided. Some professionals condemned me for knowingly playing into the militants' hands by giving them cause for violence. Other teachers thought a good thing had happened. We needed to expose the anger and contempt the community held for the school and all its staff. To some I was a fool, to others a hero, but to most a troublemaker. The militant black man who had ignited the incident rose to leave. I stopped him outside and in front of several people, including Amelia and the two yelling women, I apologized. The women continued to berate me for having "interrupted this poor man's message." Olivia, her patience at an end, snapped, "Can't this 'poor man' defend himself? After all, this whole thing started with his being a 'man' didn't it? Then let him be a man. He can fight his own battles."

We parted.

Two days later Mrs. Jones, another black area worker for the school, approached me in the corridor towards the end of the day. She looked up and down the hall and paused until sure we could not be overheard.

"Mr. Piro," she said, with quiet desperation, "you was beautiful at that meeting the other day."

"Thank you very much, Mrs. Jones. But why didn't you say that when I needed some support, like right then?"

She looked up sharply, projecting both surprise and fear.

"Mr. Piro, I lives here. You know that?"

"Naturally I know that."

"And I want to stay living. Not necessarily here but still living."

"Then who's going to do it, Mrs. Jones? I mean, who's going to clean house in this neighborhood? I can't do it. I don't have to tell *you* that none of the white staff can. Seventeen teachers have given up here and quit, including the best principal in the business. Many of those seventeen opened this building seven years ago with fantastic dreams. Where are they now?"

"The dreams?" she asked.

"The dreams and the teachers. Your individual inaction, as understandable as it is, and an apathetic community drove them away. The black staff? What can they do? As soon as they voice the slightest criticism of anyone in this community they're branded as Uncle Toms who've sold out to whitey. So they just quietly go about their business and feel guilty because they can't do more. No, they can't clean house, but they'll do a little light dusting. What we all need is strong, respected individuals like yourself to speak out."

She shook her head sadly and said, "Mr. Piro, it's like a fire. It'll just have to burn itself out. We can't fight this element. But we'll still be here to clean up their mess just like we tryin' to clean up yours now." She hurried away down the empty hall.

The next day, almost a year after the opening of *Fiddler on the Roof,* I submitted my resignation.